YOUR WORDS

YOUR HEART

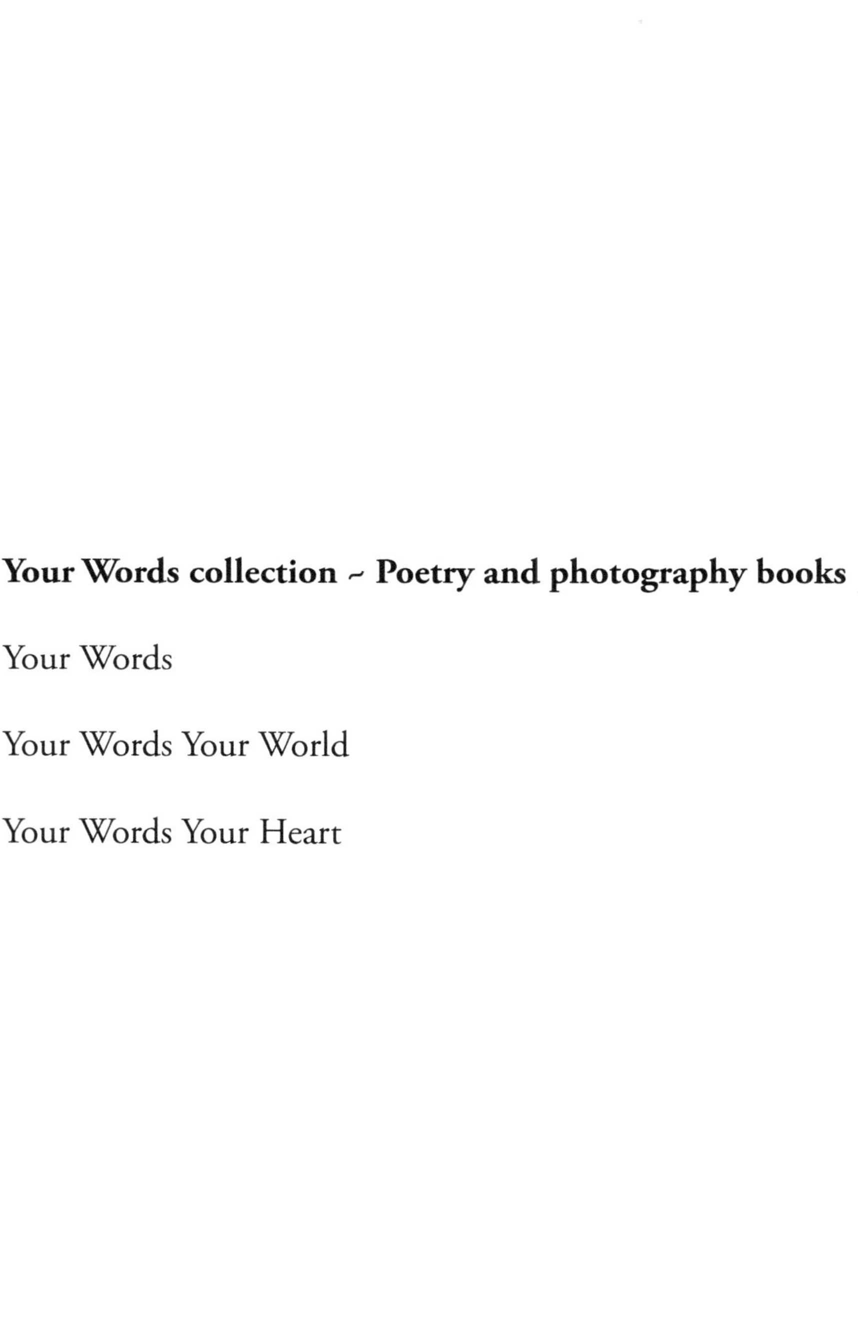

Your Words collection ~ Poetry and photography books

Your Words

Your Words Your World

Your Words Your Heart

Your Words

Your Heart

Louise Bélanger

Published by Abundance Books LLC
Kalamazoo, Michigan

www.abundance-books.com

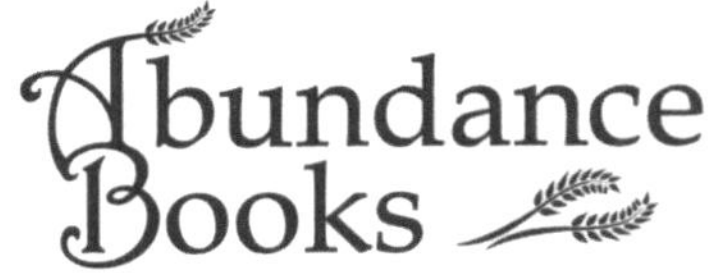

To God

To Bonnie, for your friendship and so much more

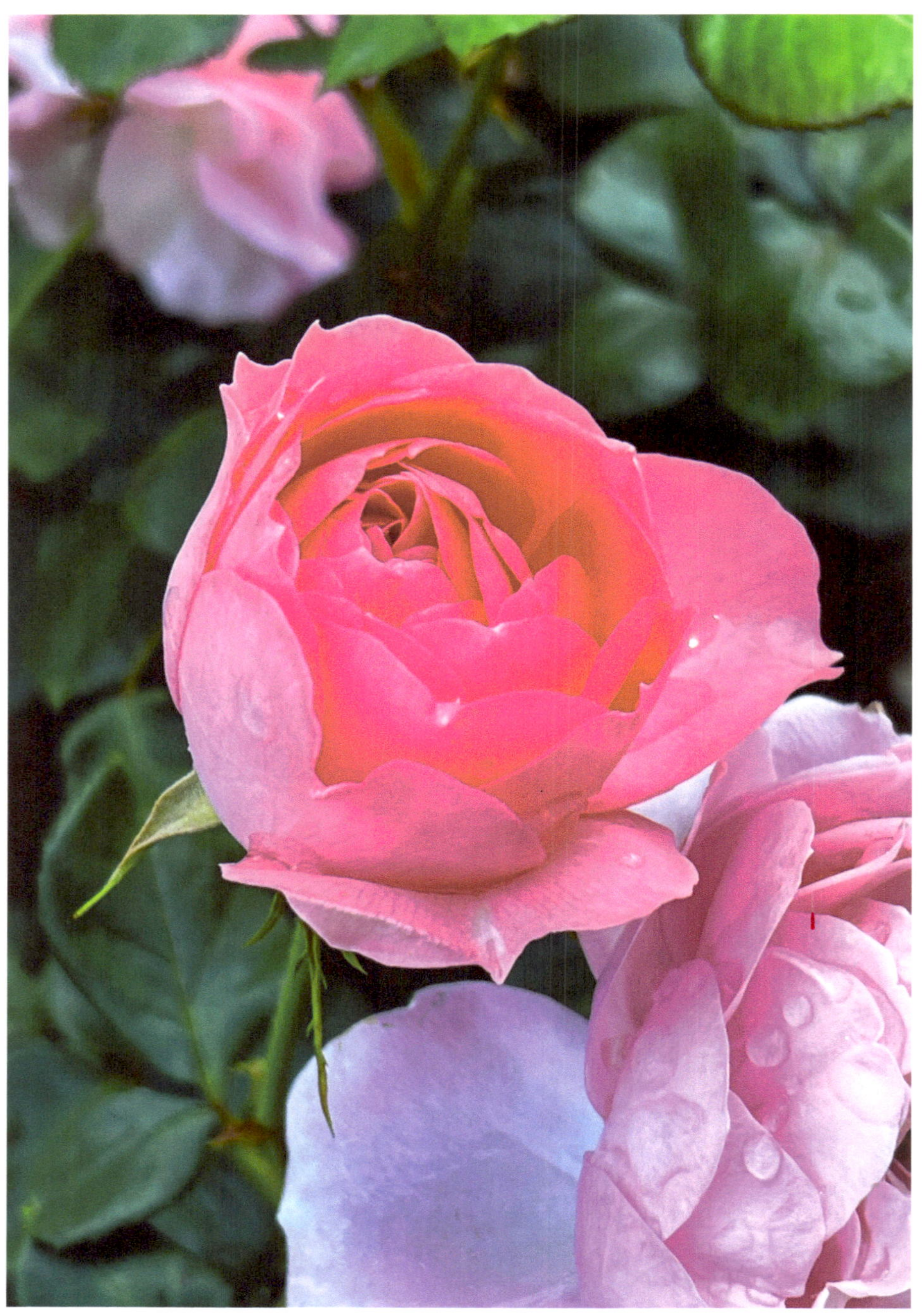

Poems, stories, photographs
All gifts from God

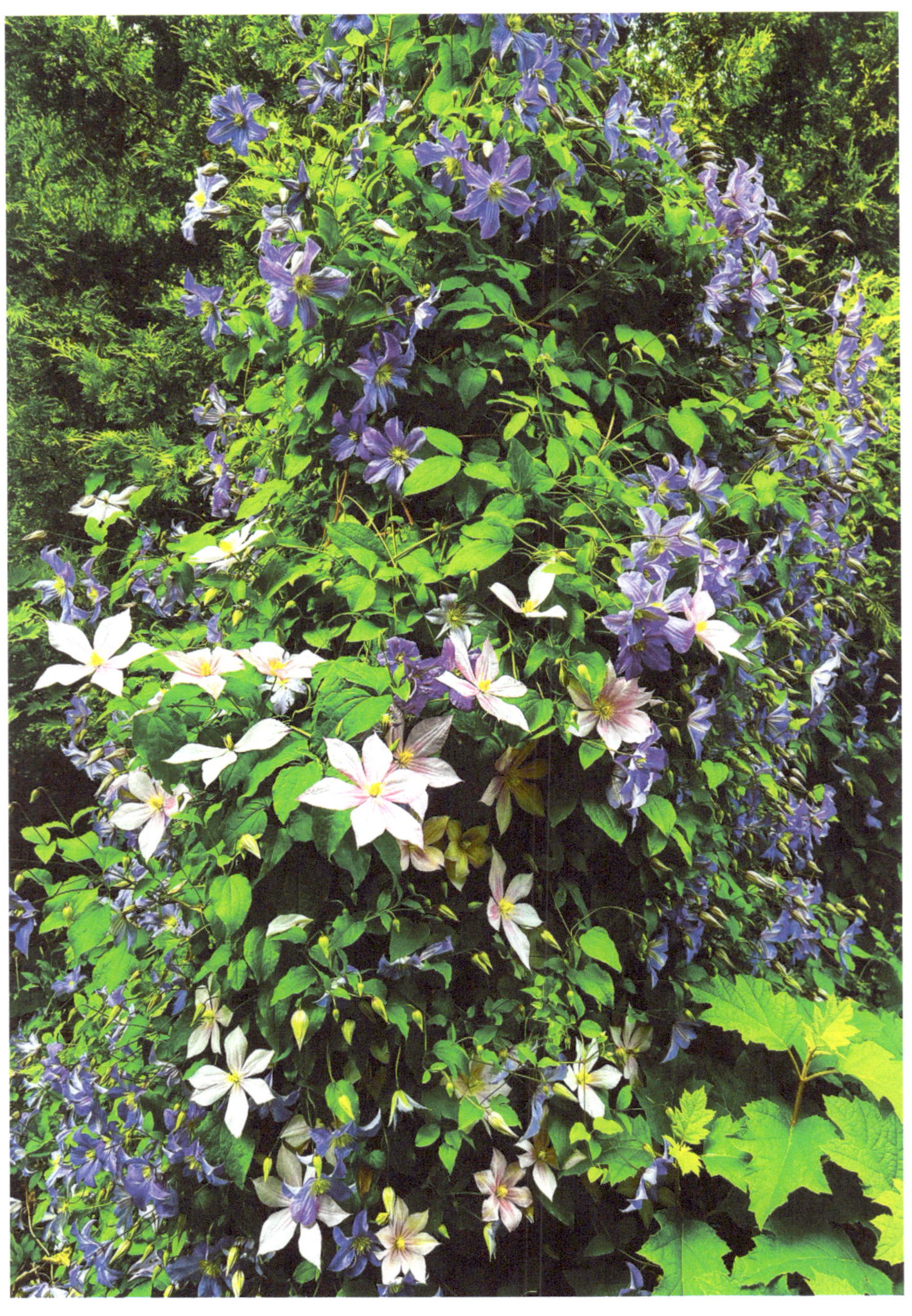

Poems

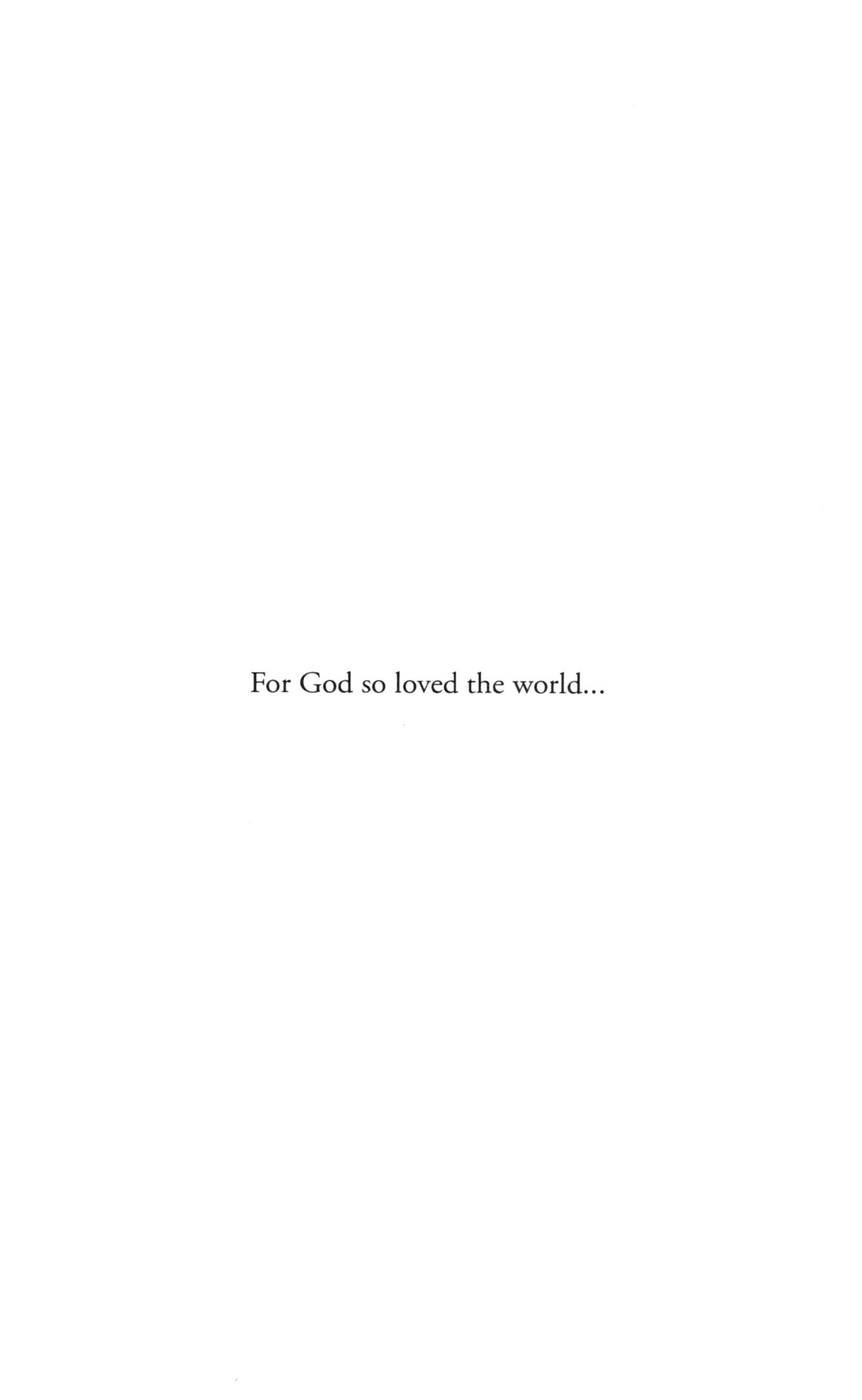

For God so loved the world...

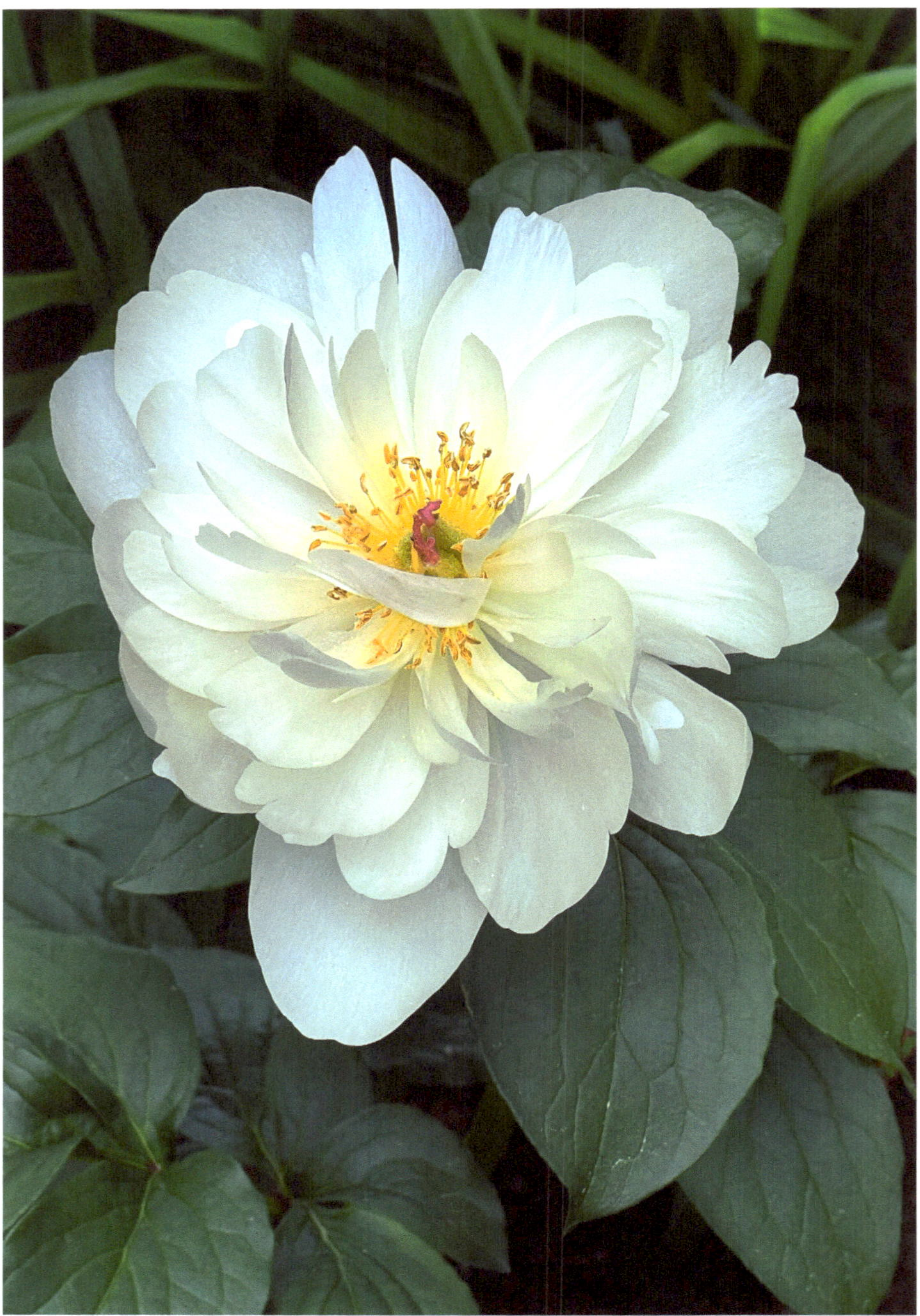

A place

A place

Where...

Judgment remains outside
And acceptance welcomes you in

The tapestry on the wall is comfort
And serenity is all you can breathe

Your soul can rest at the end of the day
And the echo you hear is love from your heartbeats

Unity is unbreakable
And loving arms embrace you

Safety and peace sit at the table
And conversations solidify relationships

A place to grow
A place to live
A place to love

A place I cherish

A place...

I call...

Home

December 2, 2021

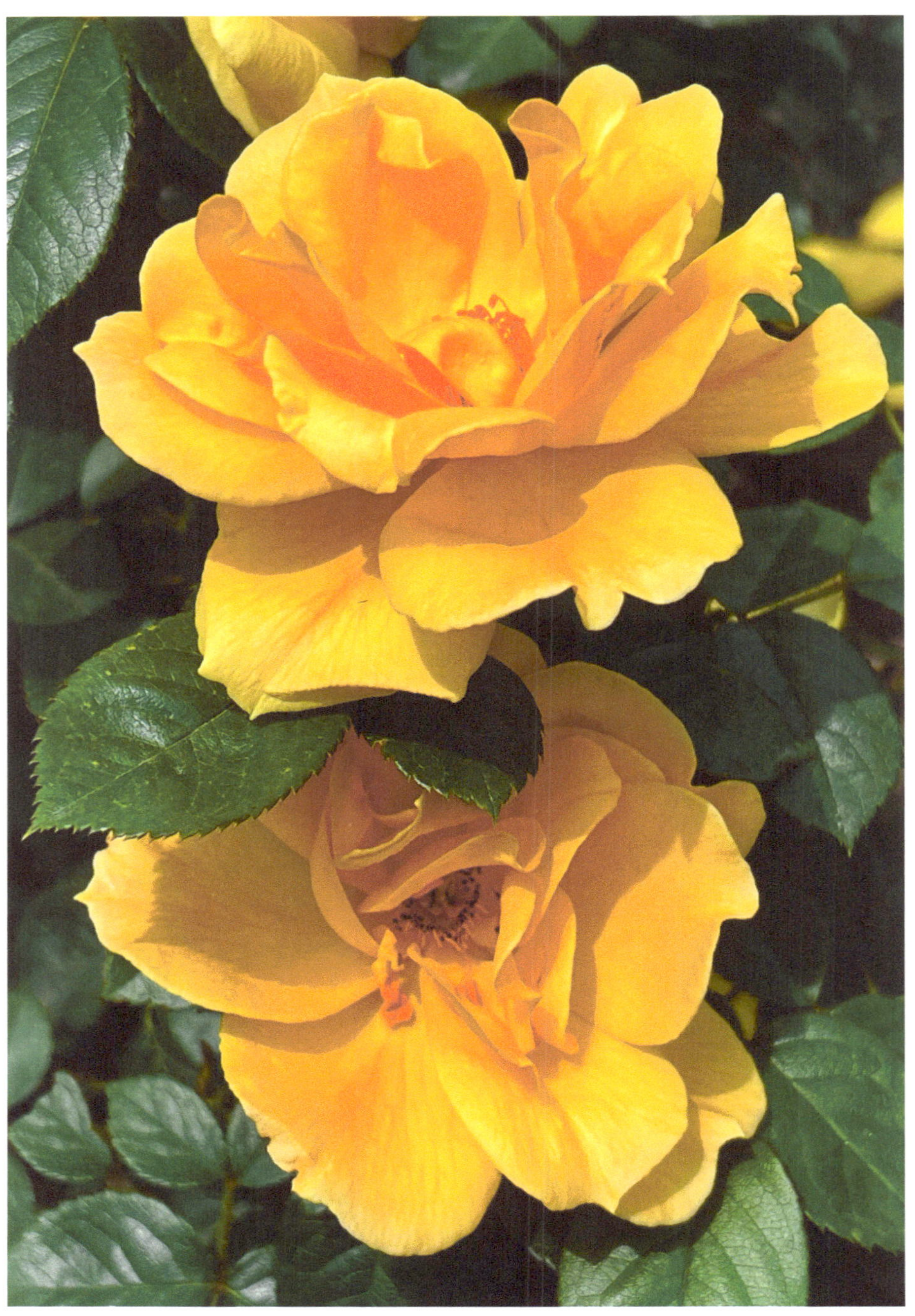

Who wins?

There is a glass
Inside of us
Where trust and doubt compete

As glass will not expand
They fight for space

Trust more
And peace will move in
Where doubt used to be

Do the reverse
And fear will invade
The room in the glass

Who wins?

It depends on what we trust
Or who?

People can fail
Trust with caution

Best to fill our glass abundantly
With the trust we have in the Lord

And among the space
Remaining
He will pour in His peace
Where doubt used to be

There is a glass
Inside of us
Where trust and doubt compete

Outside await
Fear and peace
Eager to see

Who wins?

December 9, 2021

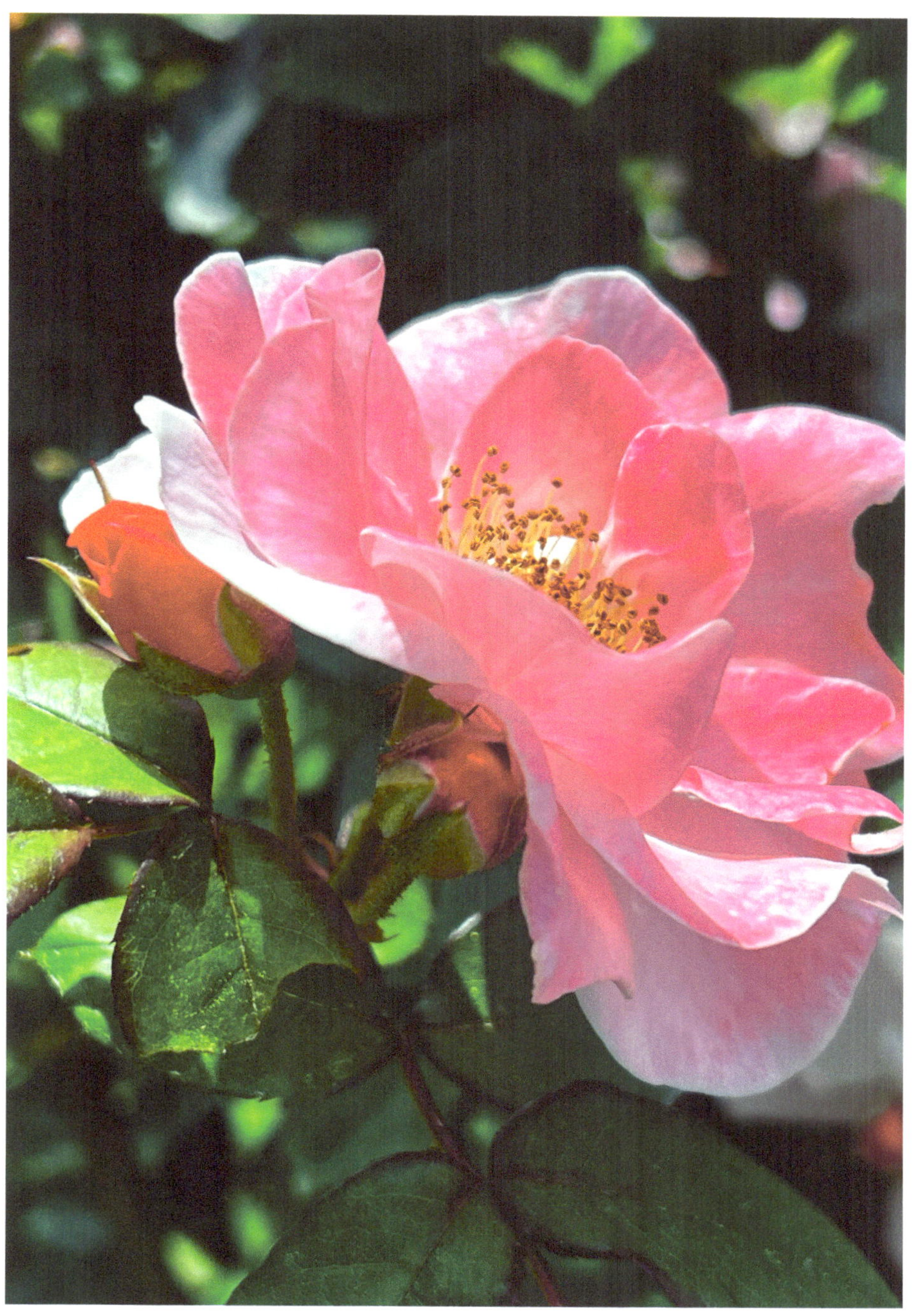

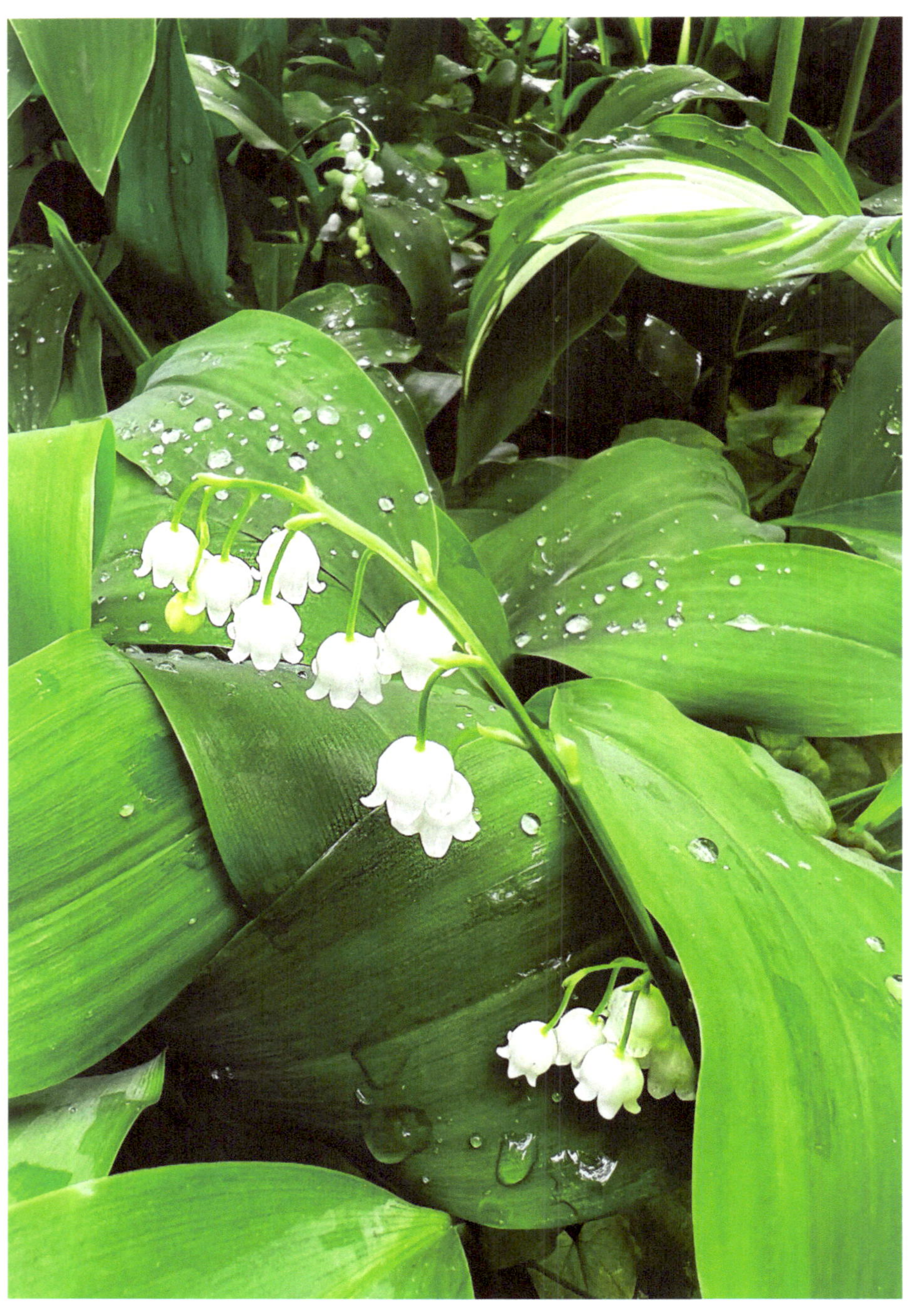

Which one...

You may look at the waves
How menacing they are

You may look at your boat
Being tossed by the wind

You may look at the blackness of the night
And how far you are from the shore

You may look at the heavy downpour
That is drenching your clothes

You can stare at your storm...

But then you will never see...

The One who's walking towards you, ready to help

The One that can rebuke the gale and quiet your sea
Your illness, your loss, your pain, your struggle...
If you only believe

Stare at your storm
Or gaze at God

Which one...

Will you magnify?

Remember that...

As long as Peter
Was looking at Jesus
A miracle occurred

And he walked on the waves

Which one...

Will you choose?

December 10, 2021

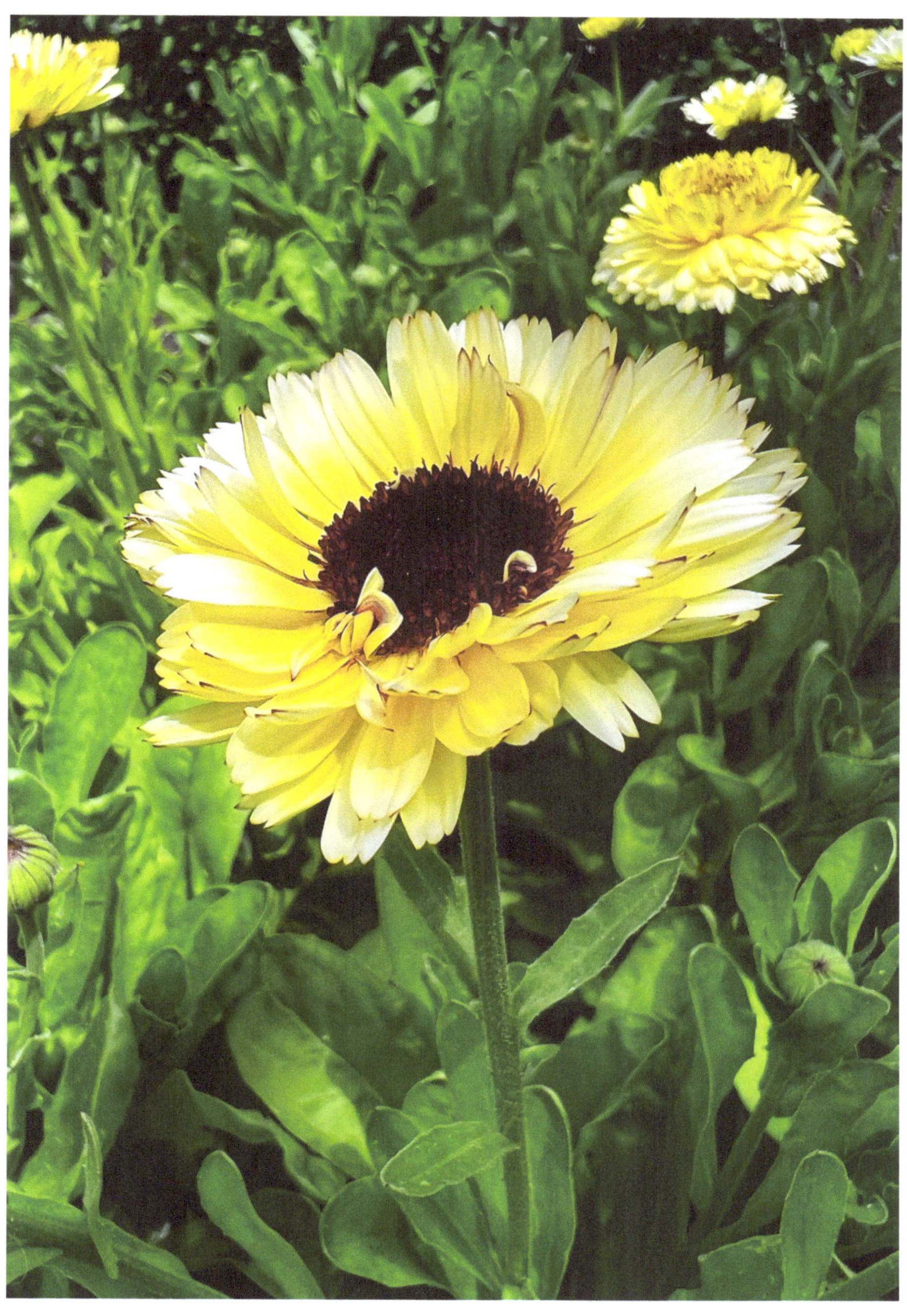

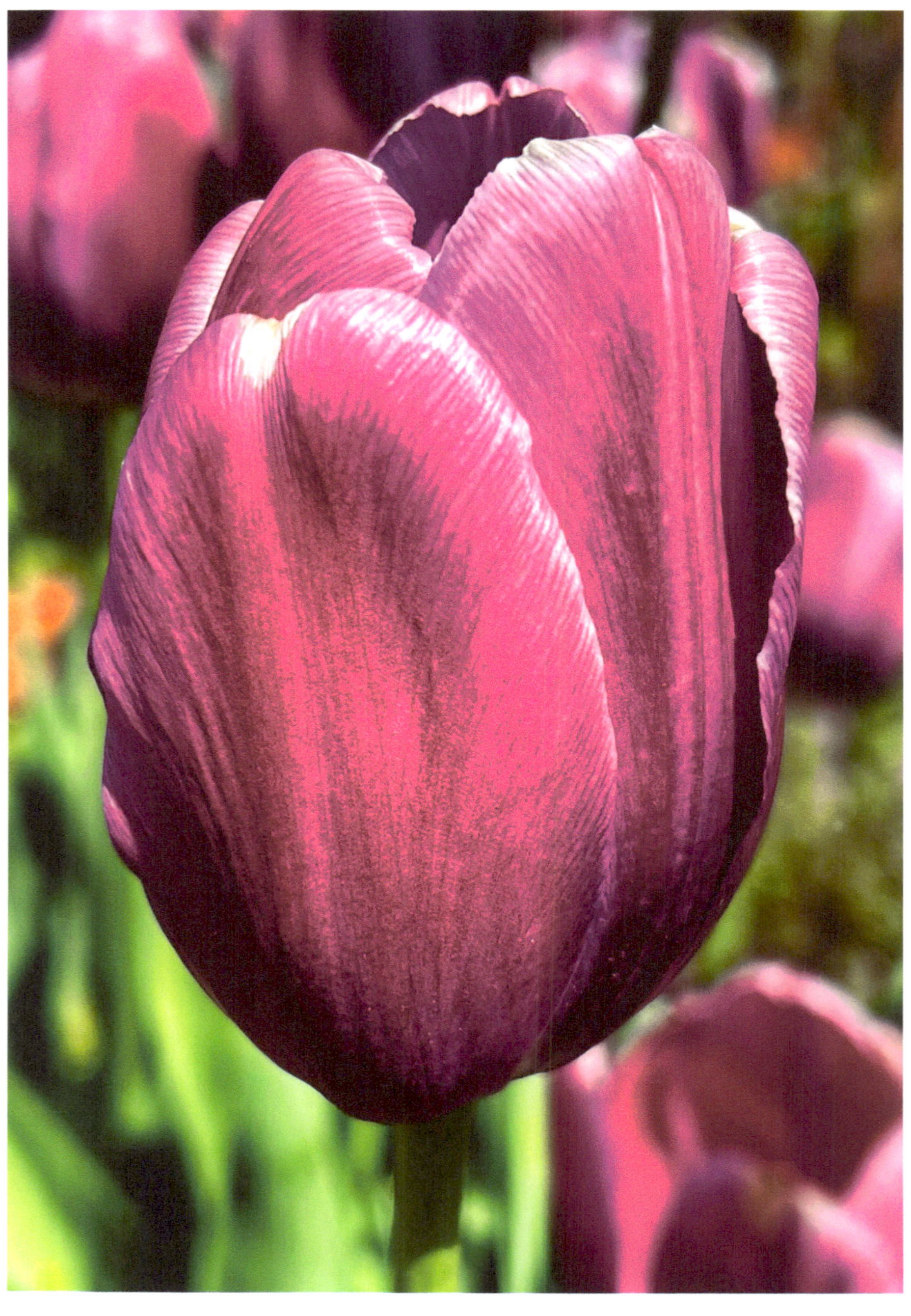

Ever

God can do
The impossible

Nothing is out of His reach
Nothing is too wonderful for Him

He can enter the world
As an infant on Christmas

Offer salvation with a cross
On a Friday we called Good

With God
All things are possible

The unimaginable goodness...
The spectacular, the breathtaking, the sublime...

My imagination can't fathom
The magnificence of His power

God can do
The impossible

Infinitely more
Than we can ask or think

Except...

Be certain
Deep down in your soul
That there is something He can't do

Don't frown at me
And stop reading
My poem

Don't frown at me
And say
That it cannot be

That you don't believe me

I assure you
Don't count on God
For one thing

God can do
The impossible

Except...

Evil

The one thing
That is impossible
For God to do

Ever

December 21, 2021

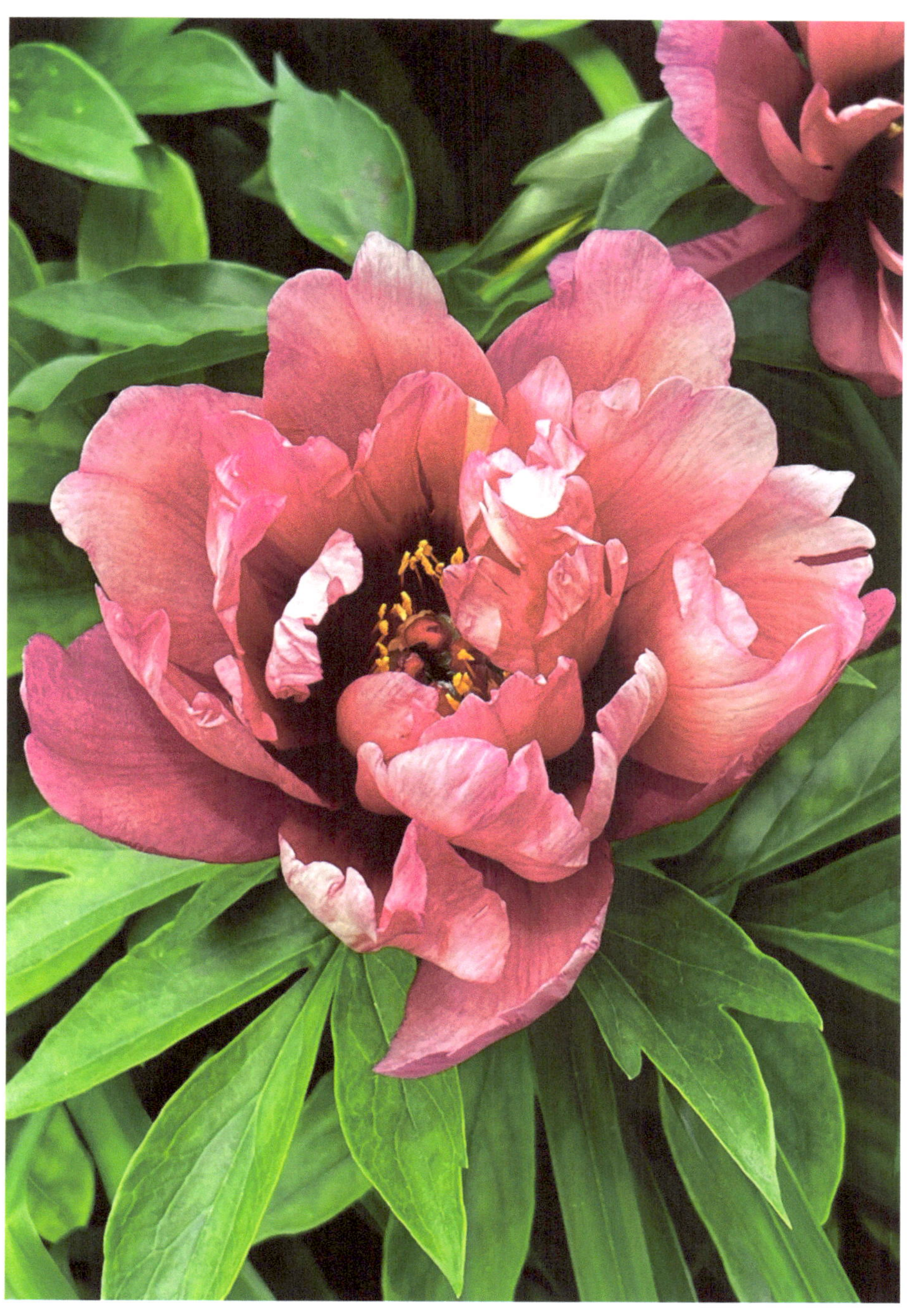

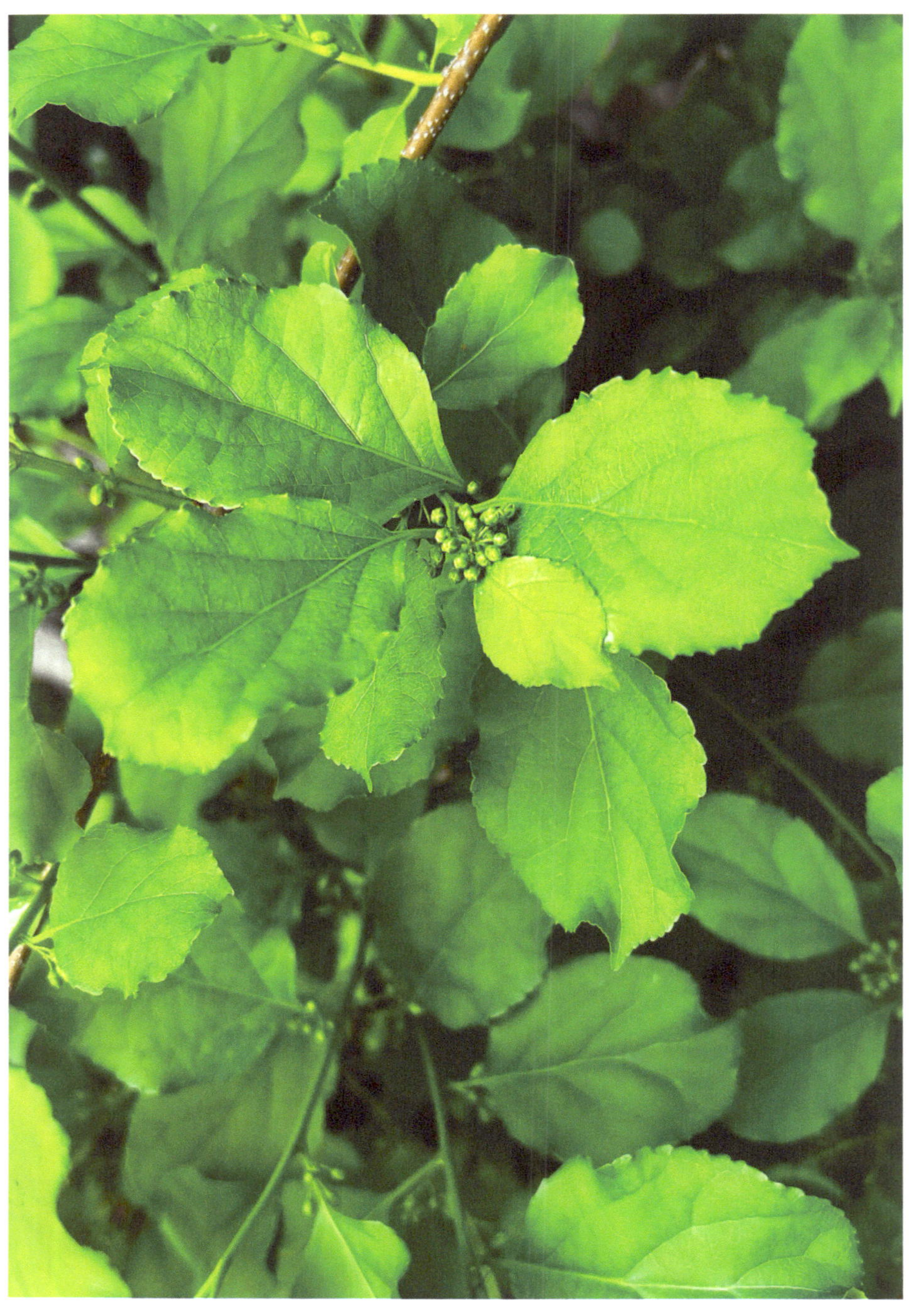

All I want for Christmas is...

All I want for Christmas is...

You

You that I adore
You who is far

You that I love
You who is lost

You that I treasure
You who is afflicted

All I want for Christmas is...

You...
That is separated
From...
Me

You that I can't forget
You that I can forgive

All I want for Christmas is...

You

My children

With Me

So I am sending my Son...for you

Signed God

December 24, 2021

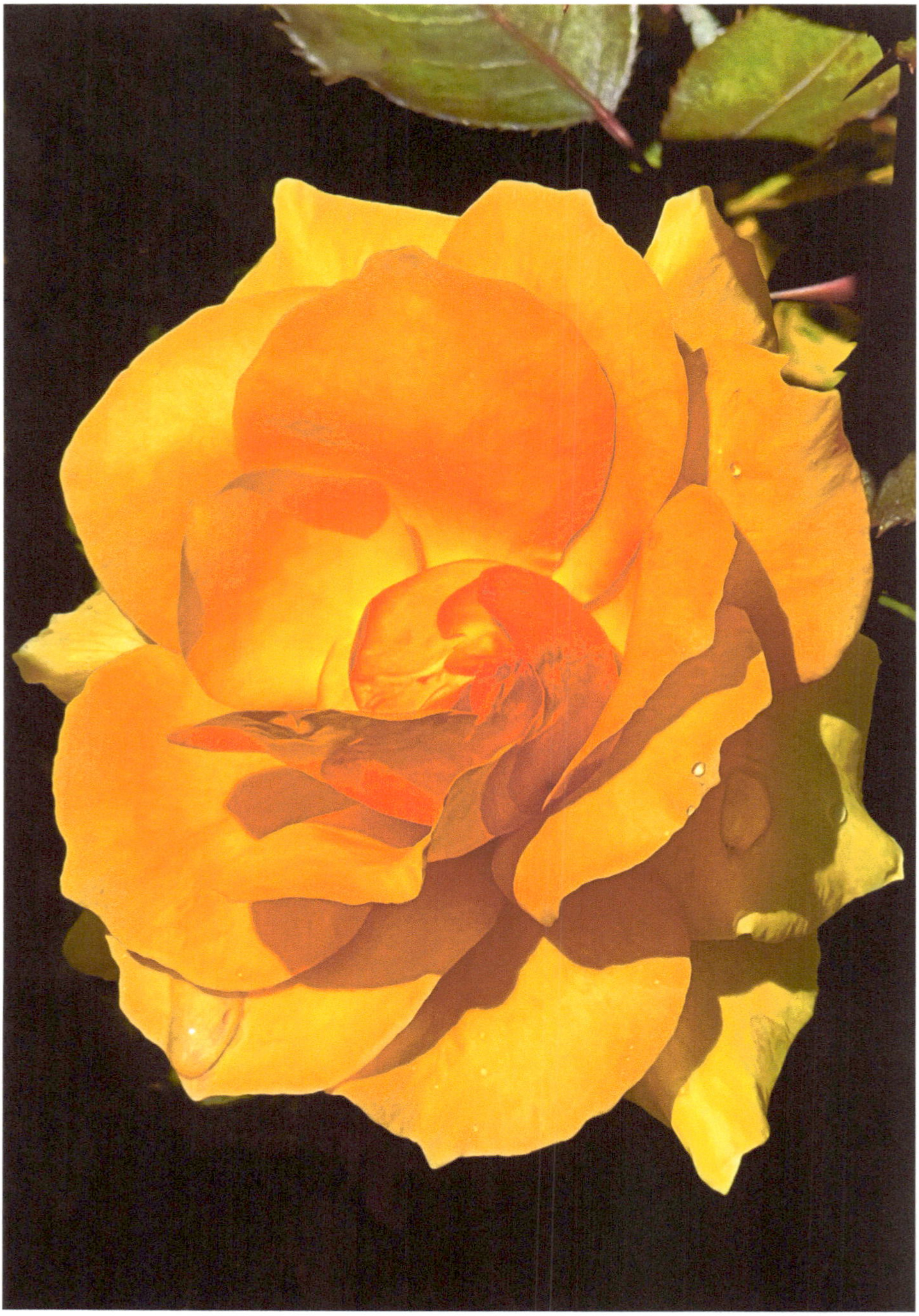

May you be kind

May you be kind

Only a few grains of sand are left

What are you hiding?

What will you bring?

What shall we remember
When you become
Just a memory?

May you be kind

The fall seems quicker now
Are all the last grains
Always eager to glide down
Towards the end?

The sky
Won't stay dark
For much longer

We will see lights

Someone has started to count

I can't see the old sand anymore

Welcome!

I see the first
Fireworks
Brightening the night

We greet you
With cheers

We greet you
With wishes

Welcome 2022!
May you be kind

May that be
How the future is
The one you hide until it becomes the past...
May that be
What you bring...

May all we remember
When you become
Just a memory...

When it's time
Once again
To turn the hourglass
For the last time
At the end of December

May we say
You've been a kind year

Welcome!
All fresh and new

How you will be
Does
Depend on us

May we be kind

So you may be

January 1, 2022

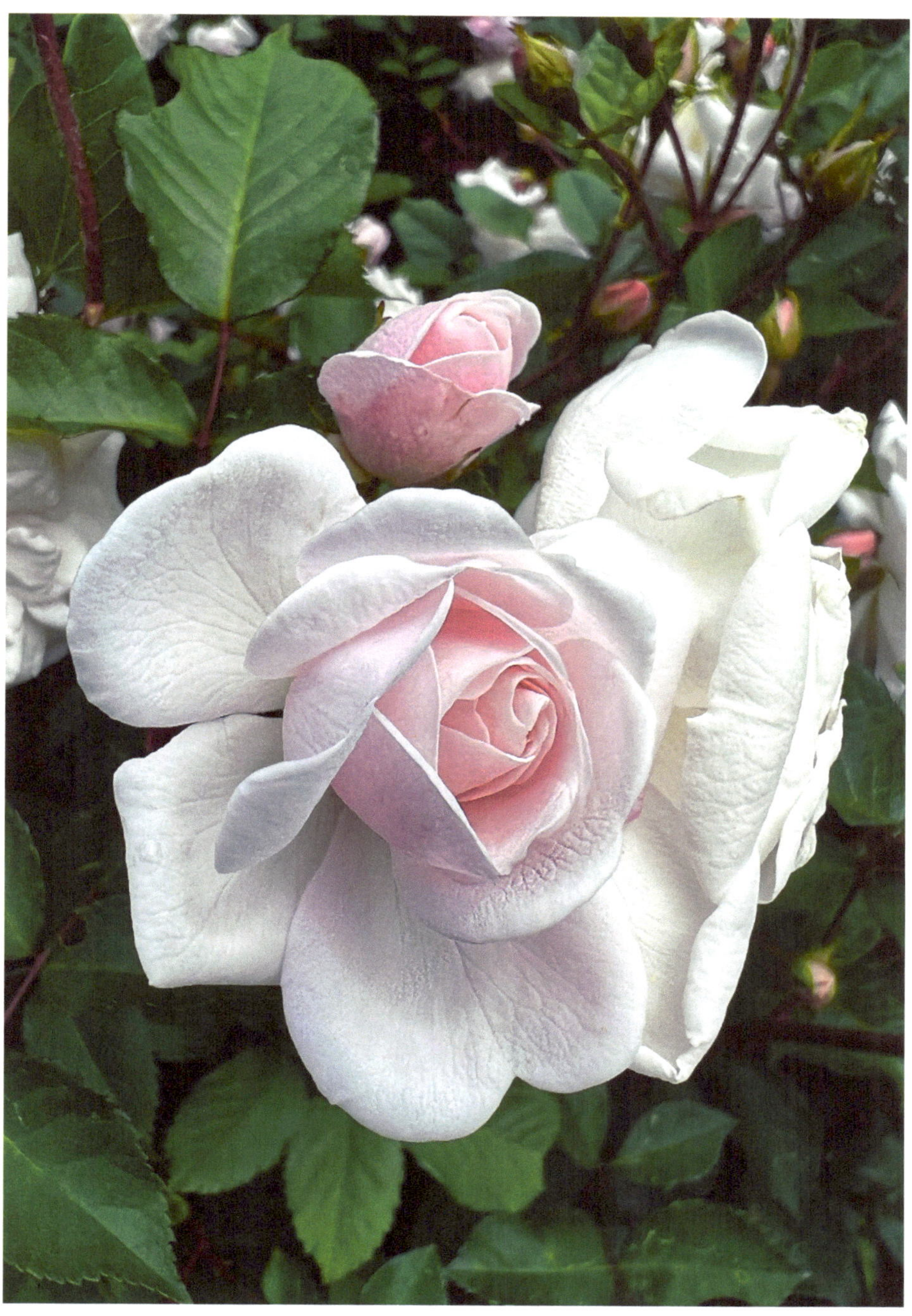

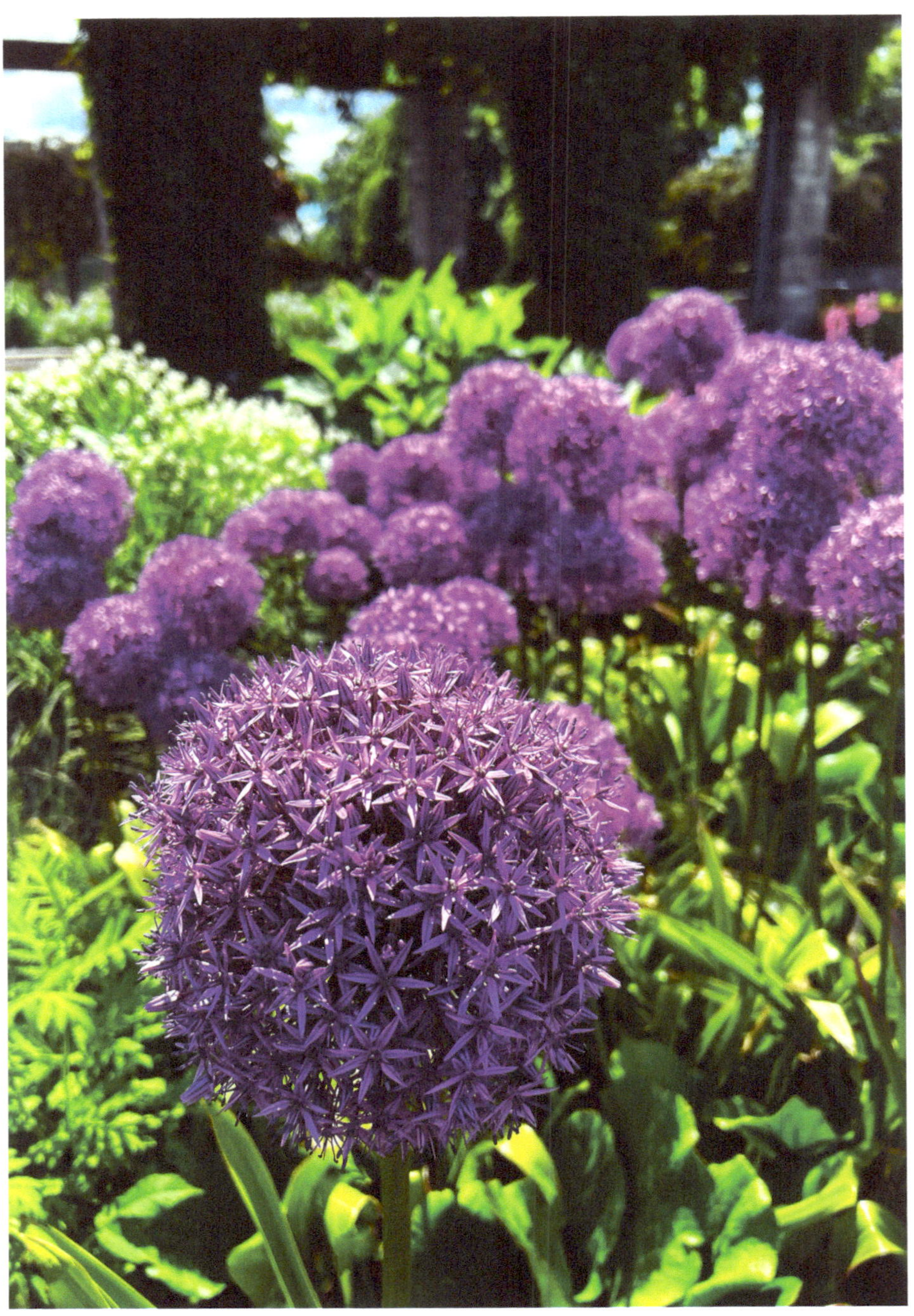

Reasons

Reasons
Behind actions
Make a difference

When we are forced to do something
The beauty of the gesture
Is lost

And there is no joy in giving
Our time, our resources, our talents
Even our smile
When we have no choice

Love...
The action word
As described in the Bible
Requires
Free will

Requires
A choice

Love is an investment
Of ourselves
Of our heart eager to do good
In our actions
Willingly
Freely

An obligation
Is not automatically love

It's a duty
We perform

It can be honorable
Depending on the task

The difference lies
In the reasons
Behind

When love
Is the motivator...

Then there is beauty
In the gesture

And joy
Will...

Invade our heart

Invade our soul

Reasons
The essence of them

Behind our actions

Make...

And are...

The difference

January 7, 2022

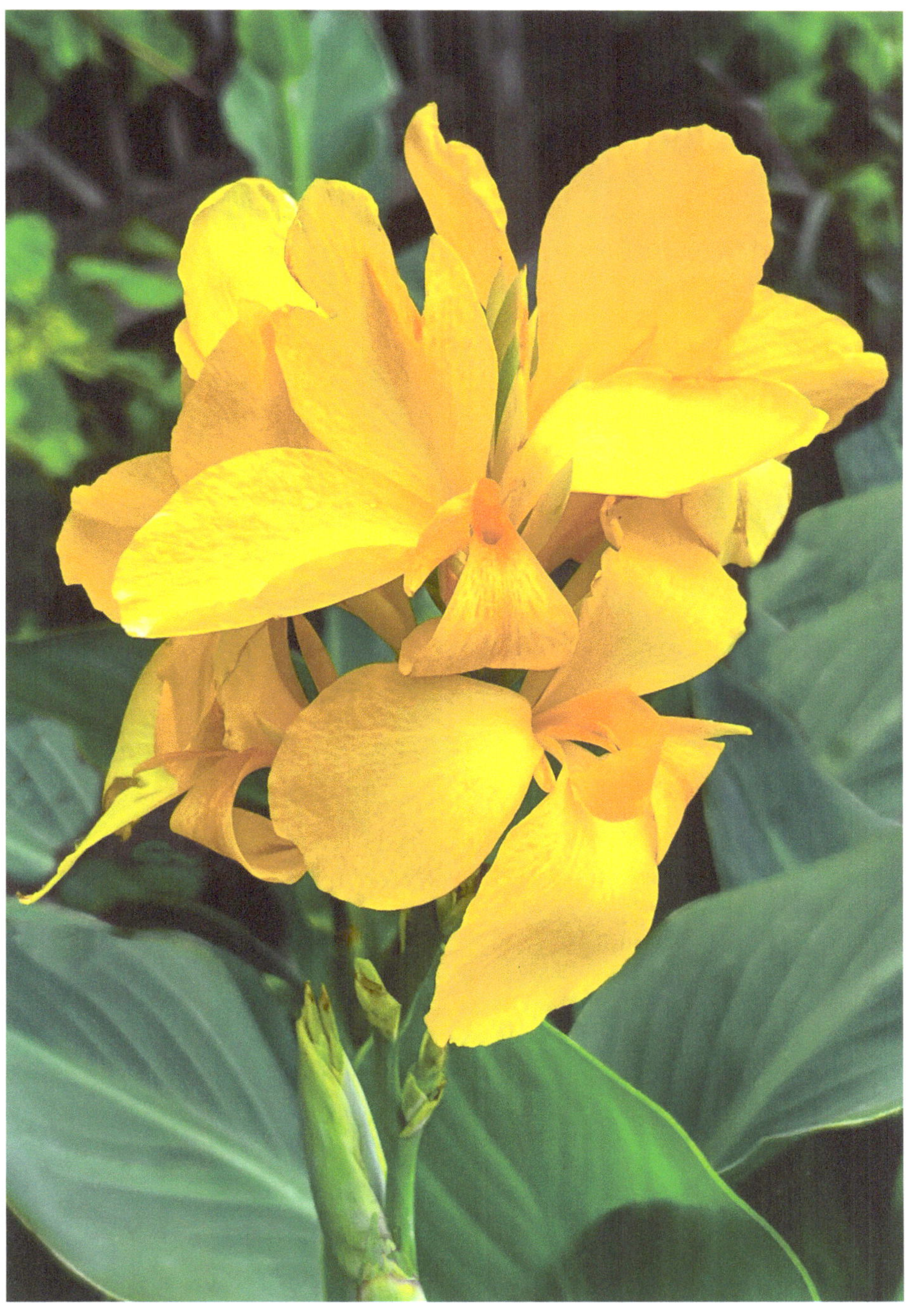

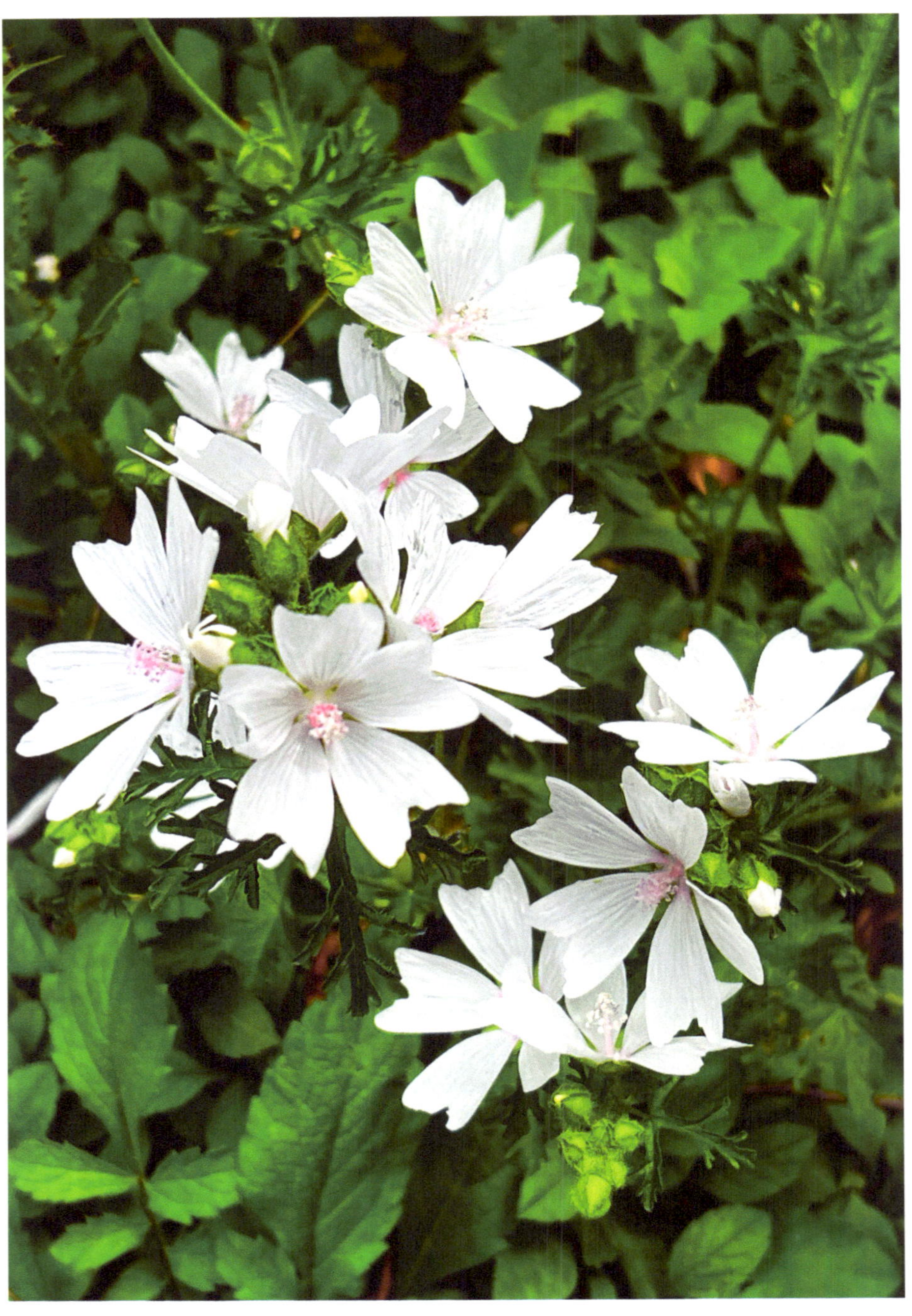

Which one are you?

Only one

Only one came back

Nine had better things to do

Too busy with selfies?
"Look at me, look at me."

Ten received

Only one came back

Nowhere
Can we read
How that
Made
You feel

Disappointed?
Maybe sad?

Or was it deeper?
A hurt
A pain
Inside
Your heart

I know I would
Have felt that
If it would have been me

Especially
Since the disregard
The indifference
Came from loved ones

And it did...

Because
You
Love them all

All ten

Lepers
Foreigners
Pleading with You
Begging
For healing

The miracle
Was granted

Ten received
Ten were healed

But only one came back

To worship You, Jesus
To give thanks to God

What about you?

Which one are you?

The one that comes back?

Or part of the nine
Who always has
Better things to do

Better than
Take time to give thanks
To God

For all that He has given you
Done for you

What about
When you plead and receive?

What do you do after that?

Ten were healed that day
From leprosy

Only one came back
To worship
To give thanks

And only that one
Was saved that day

Because of his faith

Which one are you?

January 12, 2022

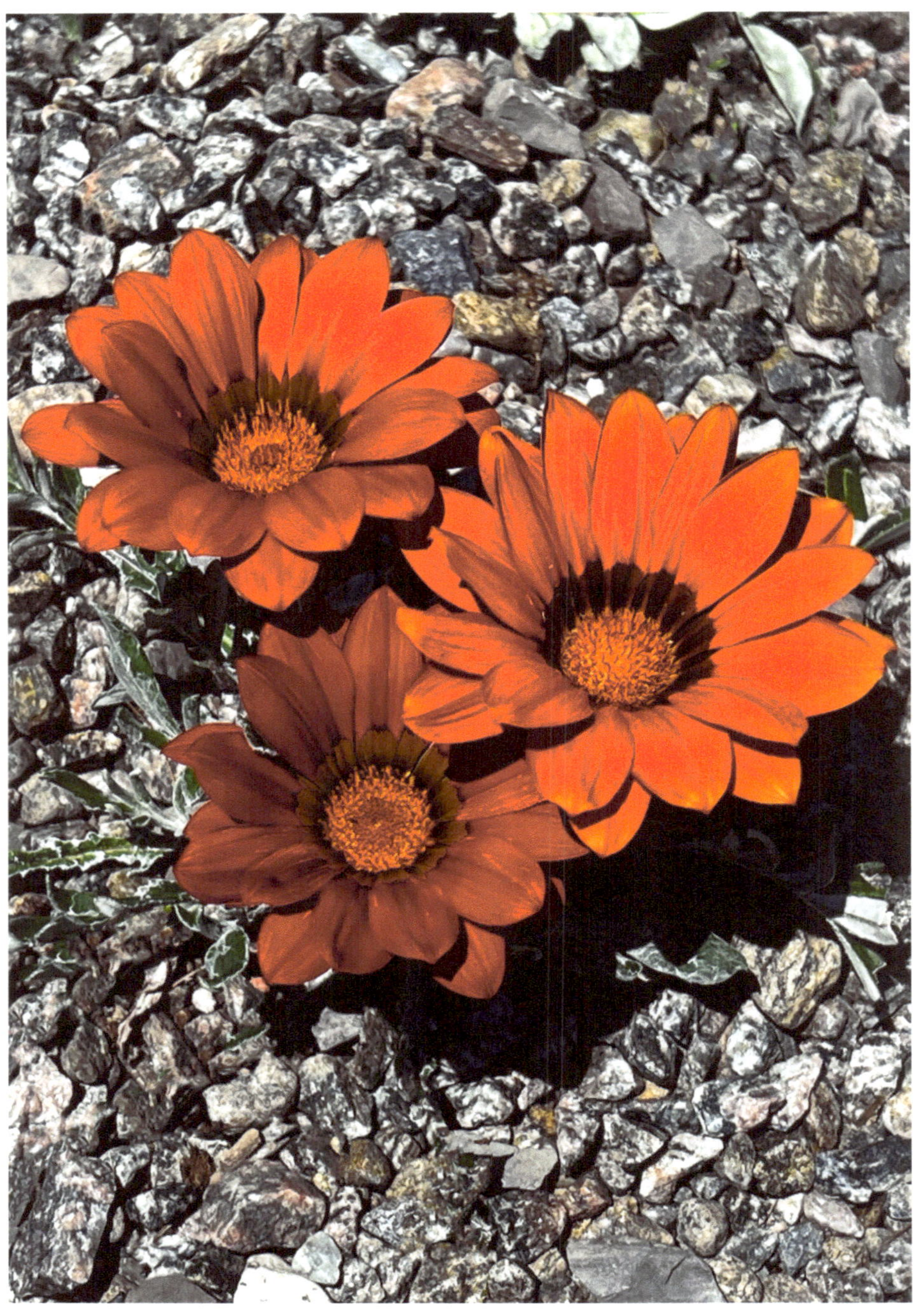

"How much does it cost?"

"How much does it cost?
I have three dimes in my pocket."

"You can't pay with dimes."
He answered

"I work hard."
Replied the child
"How many weeks of chores will be enough?
How much does it cost?"

"You can't pay with works."
He explained
"None can be worth the cost."

"And the price has already been paid."

Wide eyes
The child wondered
How?
Who?

So the teaching began

And the child...

Understood...
Believed...
Repented...
Received...
Trusted...
Followed...

The Son
The Teacher

The One who paid the price

For us

Because we couldn't

A price
That can't be paid
With dimes or millions
Chores or works

A price
Only Jesus could pay

And He did

Out of love

Let Him teach you

Let Him tell you

Ask Him

"How much does it cost?"

January 19, 2022

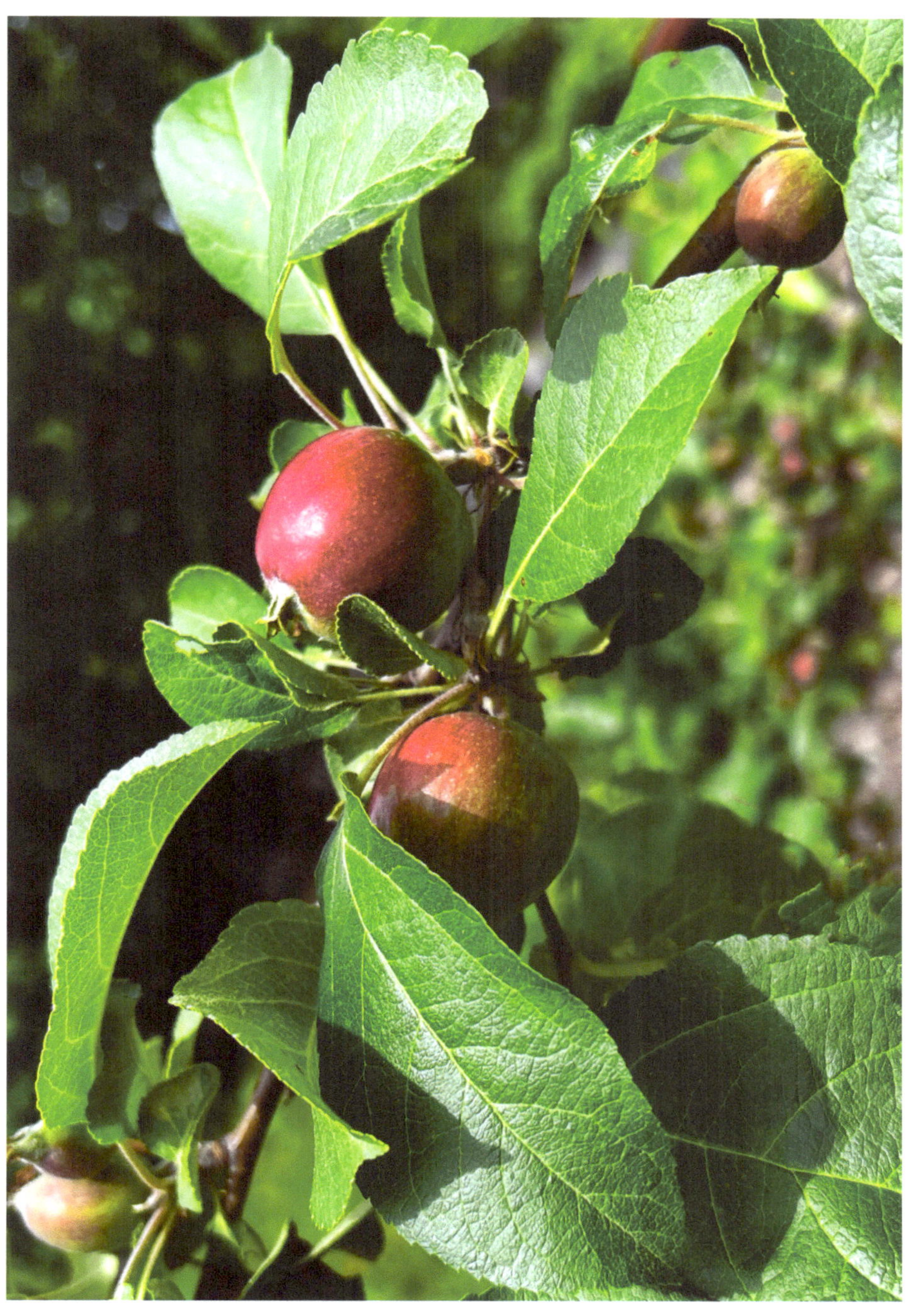

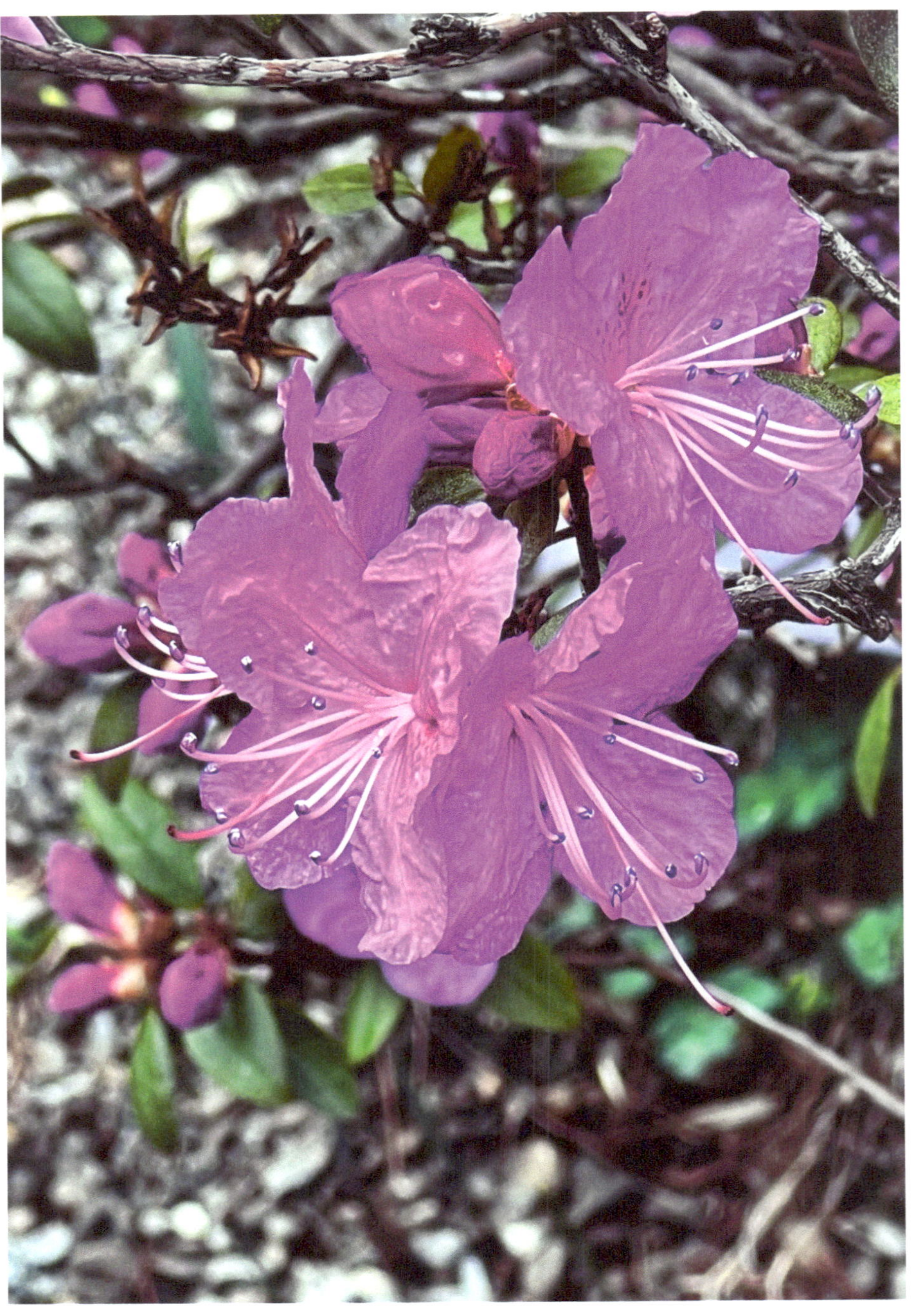

What do you see?

What do you see?

Some saw a criminal
Someone who got what he deserved
Someone caught disobeying the law, the rules...and rightly punished

A spectacle
As a warning to others
This is what happens to bandits
Beware

What do you see?

The end of the threat
Against the authorities?

Against the people?

Or a beloved
Who took our place?

What do you see?

When you look at the cross

February 3, 2022

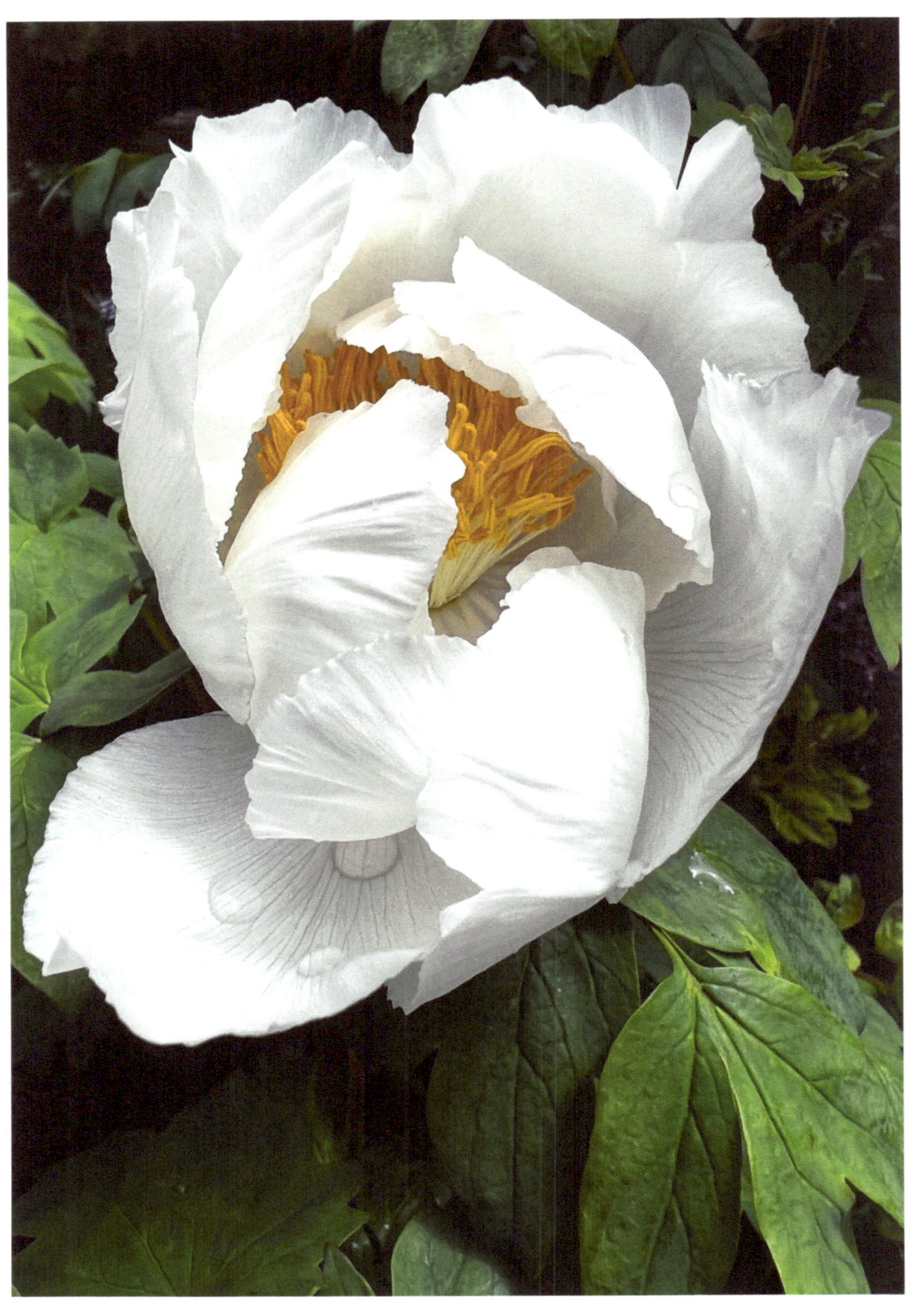

Petals like hearts

Petals
Like hearts
Are subject to frost

A change in the wind

In the natural for one
More complex causes for the other

And edges turn into ice

Unattended
With time
The cold
Infiltrates
The core

Crystalizing

The no longer soft

Petals

Hearts

The sun can warm one

The Son can heal the other

Petals
Like hearts
Are subject to frost

February 4, 2022

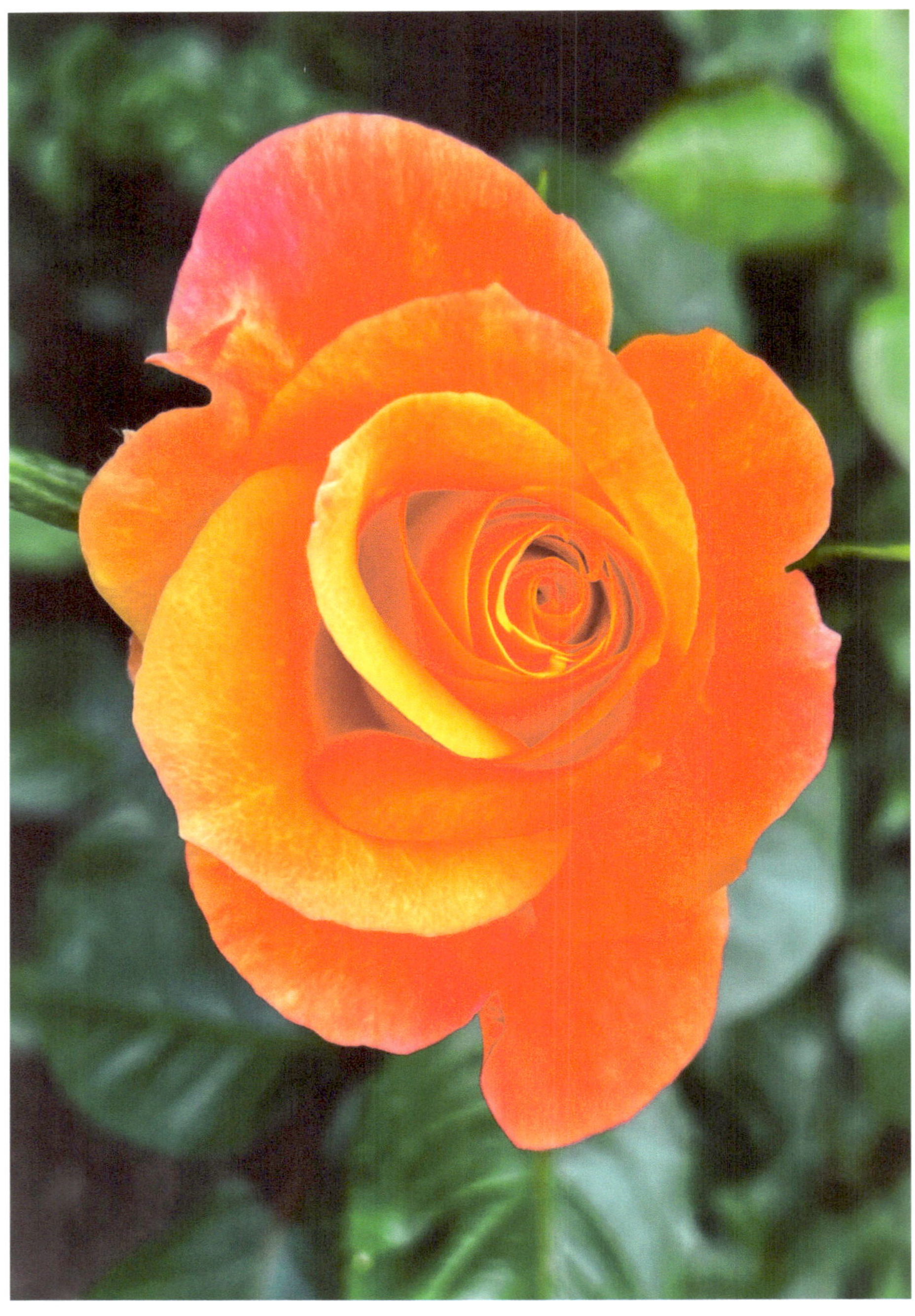

Ripple effect

Ripple effect

We see it on the water
As it swallows the stone

We see it in the world
As it does the same with our actions

Construct
Or destroy

Encourage
Or push down

Consequences

Good or bad

Ripple effect

We see it every day in someone's life
As it swallows words, gestures, behaviour...
Silences, anger, kindness, neglect...
Acceptance, selfishness...
From others

Ripple effect

Don't create
Damaging ones

Take a stand

Control the circles

Look at the stone
Before you throw it in

Before someone

Before the world

Swallows it in

Make sure it's good

Ripple effect

We see it on the water

We see it everywhere

Every day

In this world

Consequences

Good or bad

February 10, 2022

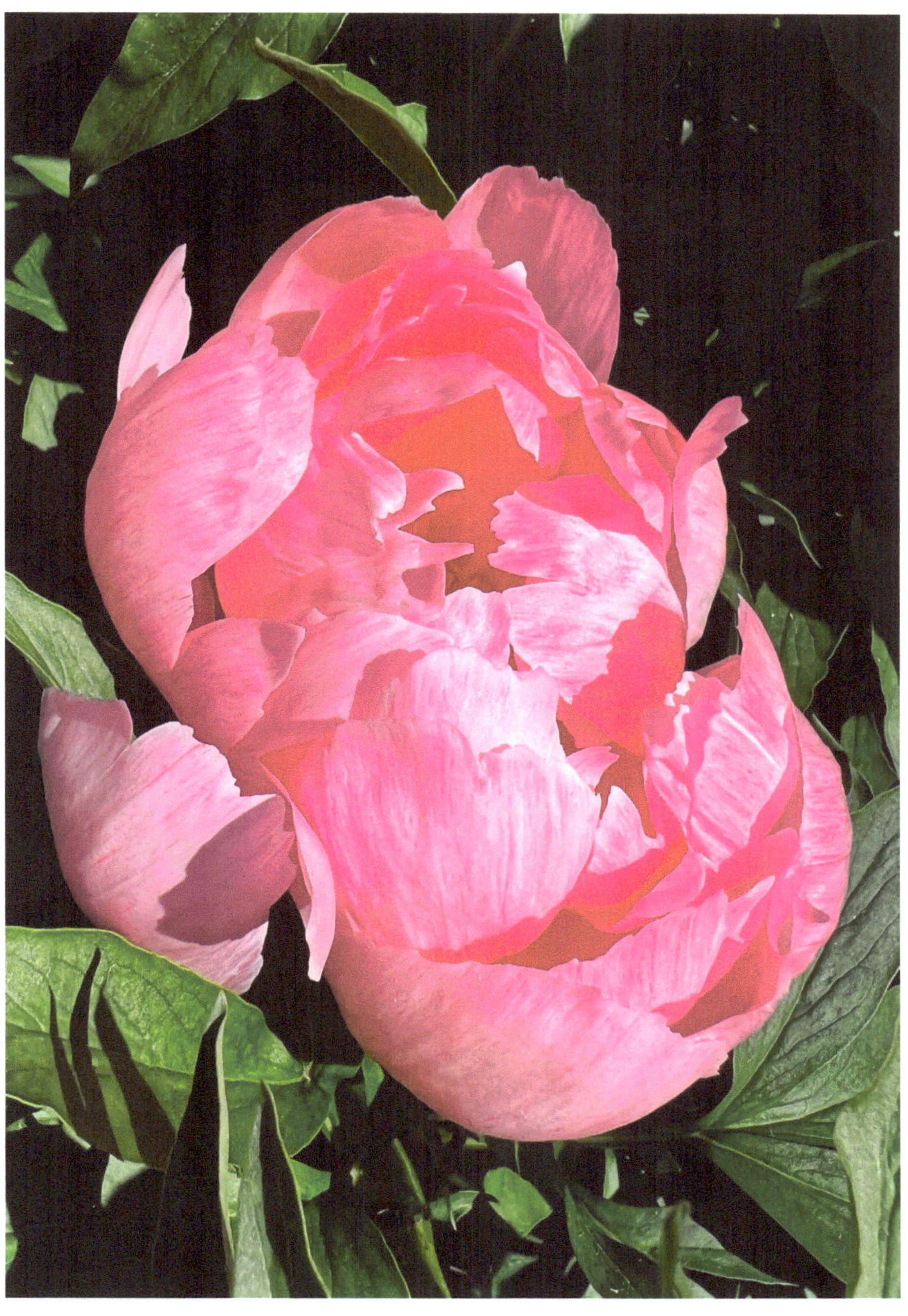

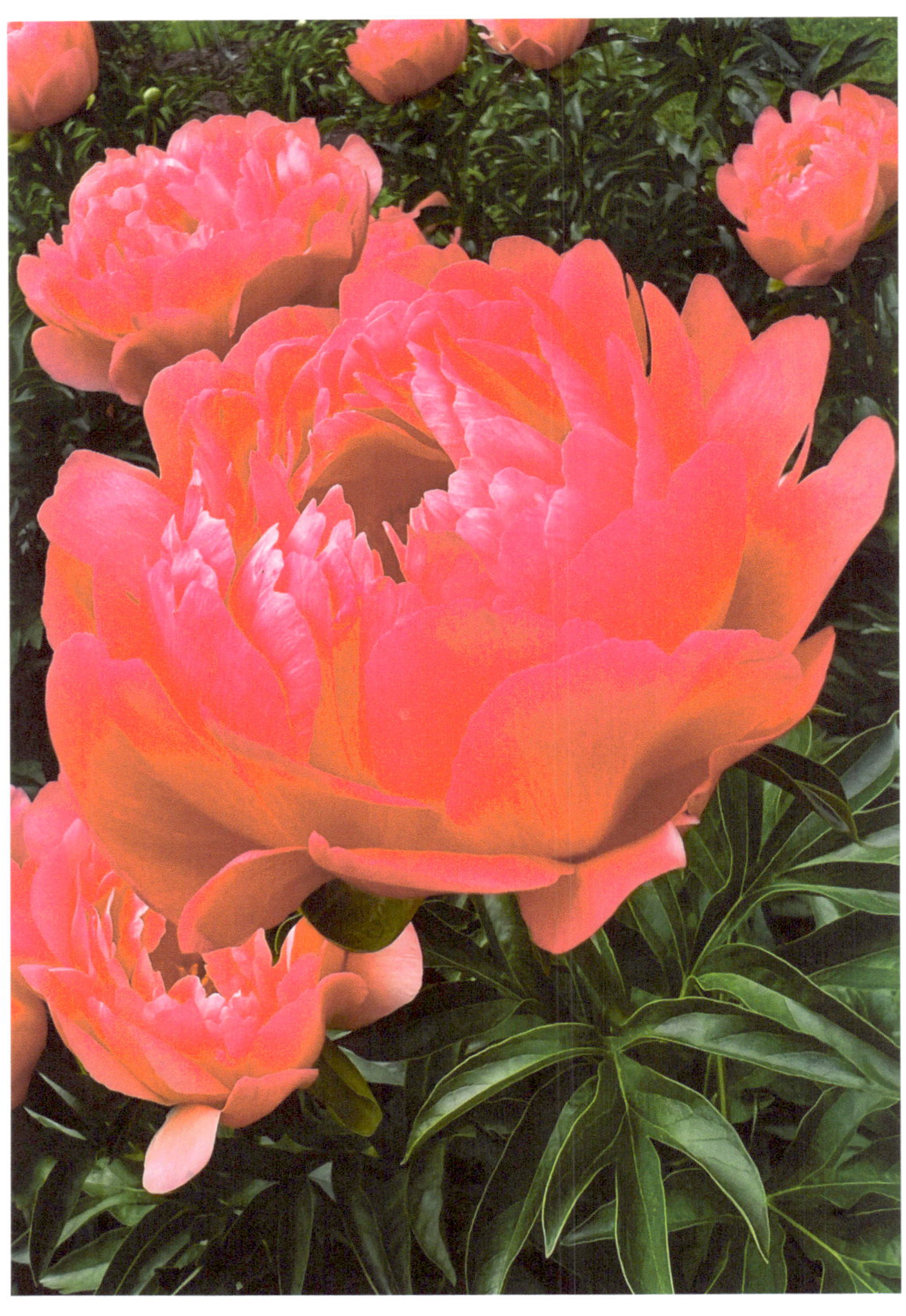

Steadfast love

Steadfast love

Immovable
Never-ending

In a world
That's always changing

Don't we need a rock?

In a world
Where feelings
Come and go

Don't we need faithfulness?

Don't we need a love
That never dies?

A fiercely burning love
Continuously

Never wavering
Even when we fail

A love we can anchor our life to

A love we need

The love You give

February 19, 2022

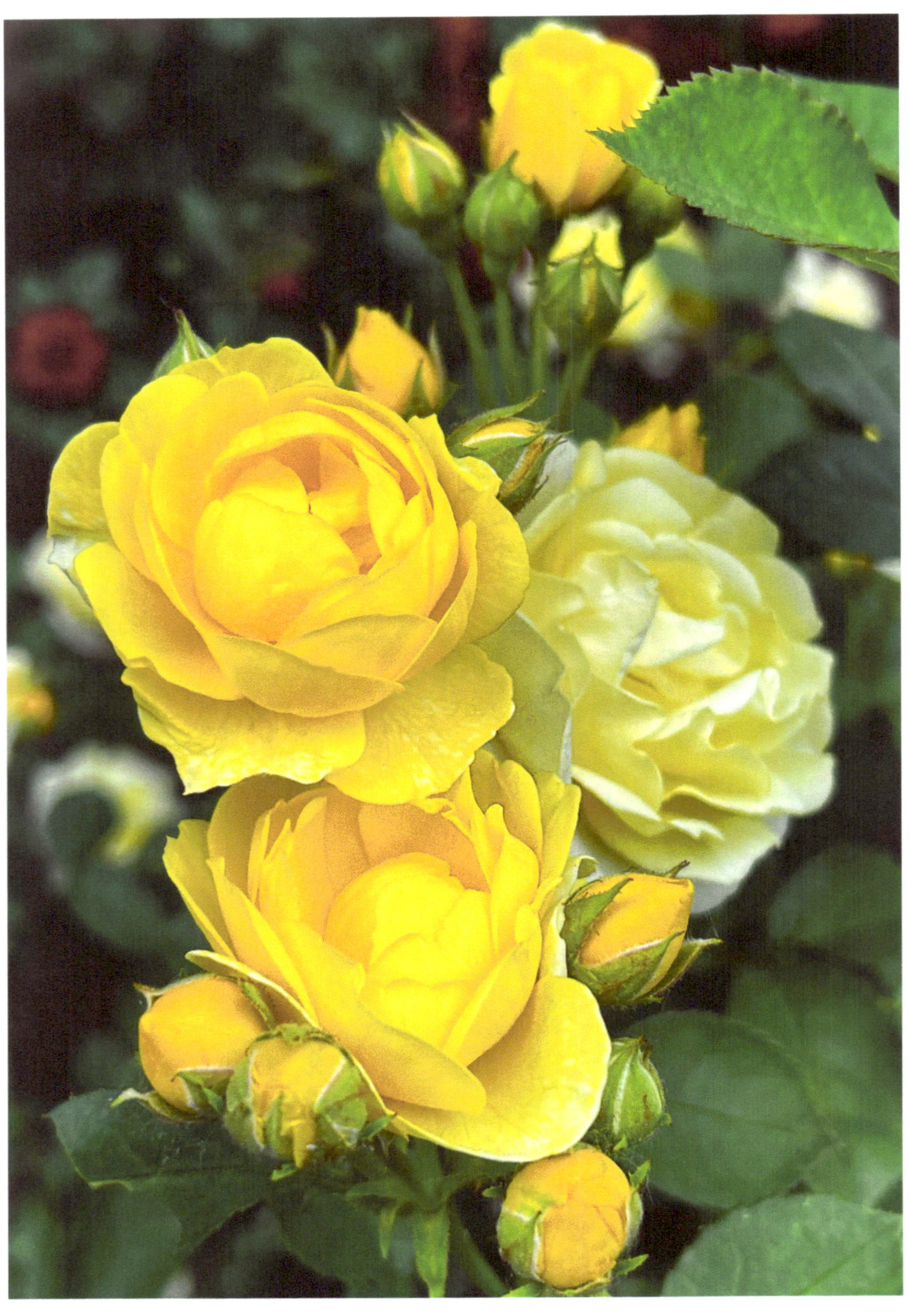

The intruders

An intruder
Has entered

And the attack begins

Layers
Upon layers
Are applied

To mobilize

To neutralize

Completely changing
Its appearance

Eventually

Becoming
Like the wall
Of its prison

Resting
In the softness

The intruder
Is now...
A beautiful pearl

Locked
In the shell

Love covers a multitude of sins
The Bible says

Like pearls?

Layers
Upon layers

Of grace
Of mercy
Of forgiveness...

Of love

Completely changing
Their appearances

In the softness
Of our hearts

February 22, 2022

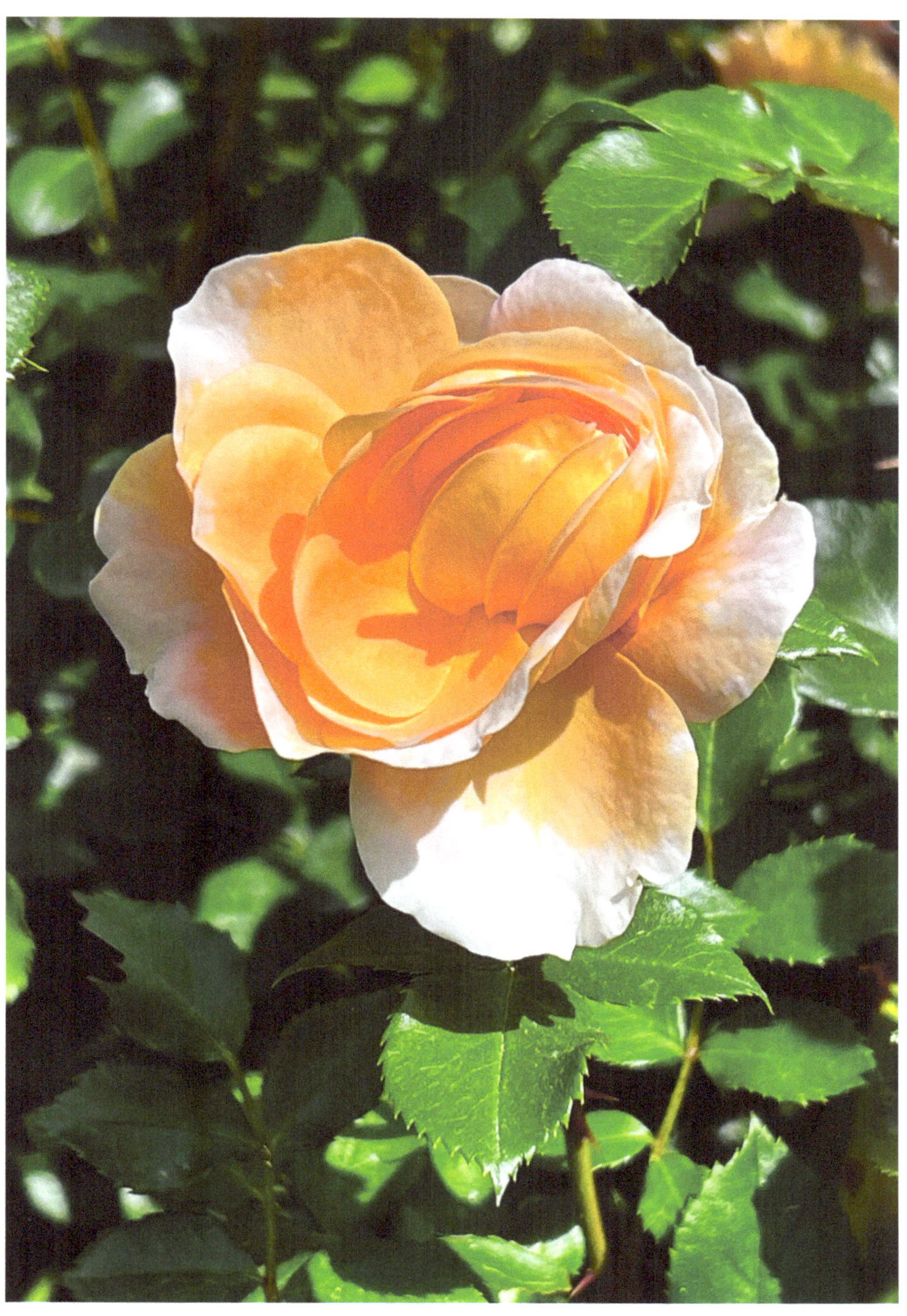

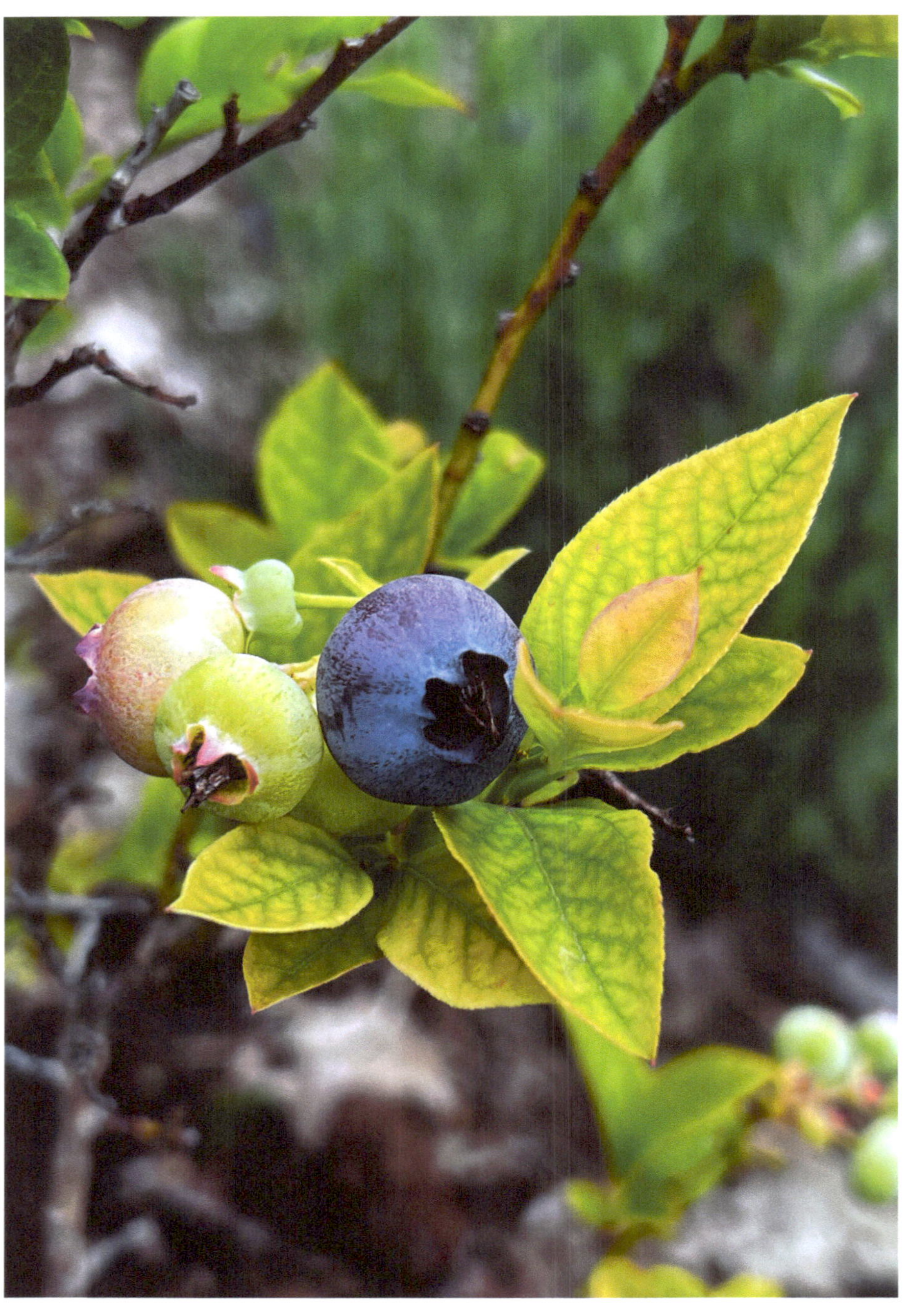

Tinsel

Sideways hat
And a frozen nose

Blind eyes
With a permanent smile

He prefers cloudy days and cold nights
To the power of the rays at midday

Three buttons hold
The invisible coat
And the wind swirls
Around his scarf

Feet buried deep
In the white surroundings

A snowball just swishes by

Giggling children
Running with wet mittens
Hurrying to add
The final touch
To the freshly made
Snowman

Tinsel

The one with the crooked hat
And a carrot for a nose

Preferring the cold
And the falling snow
To the melting power
Of the rays at midday

March 4, 2022

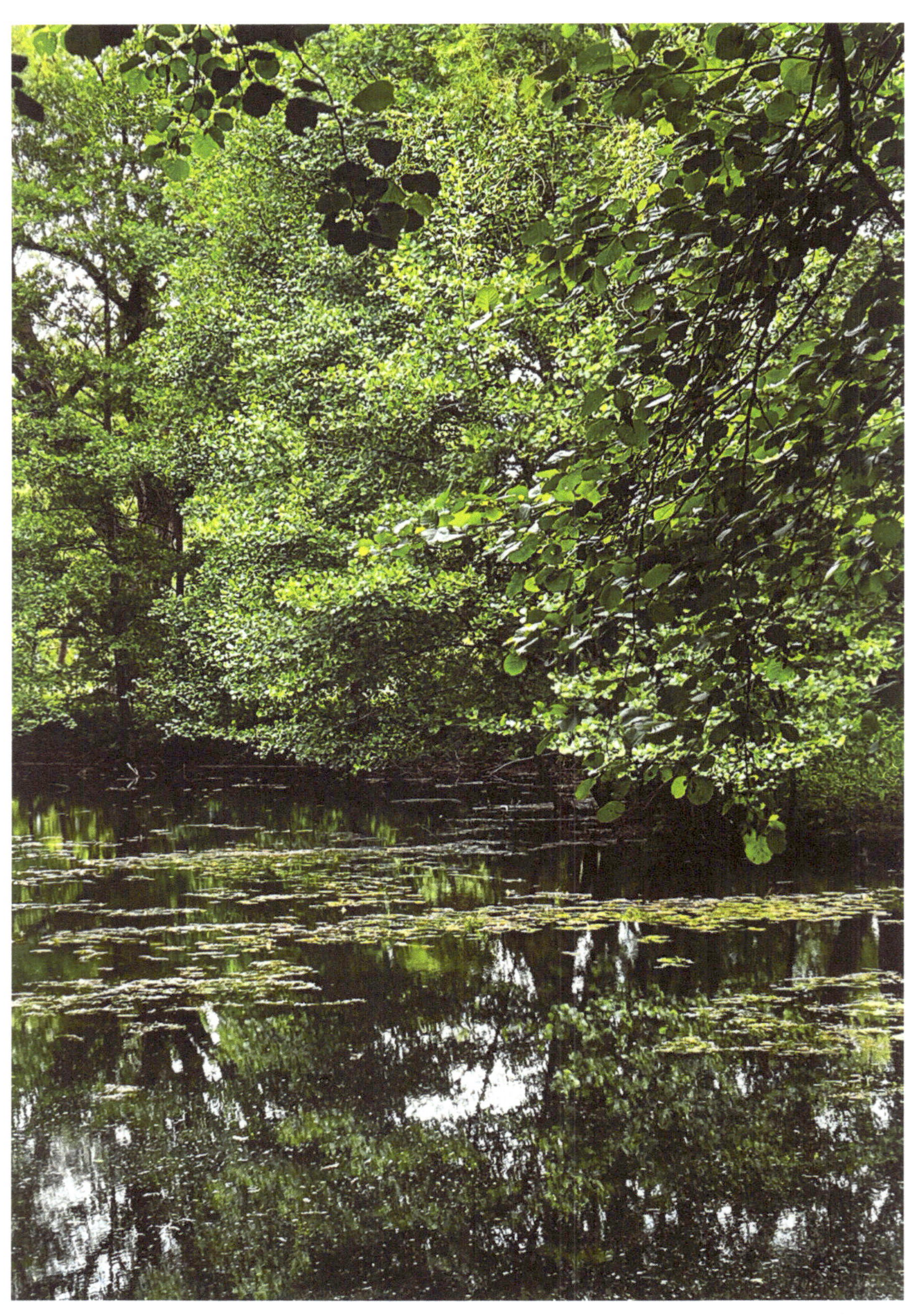

Reflection

Like a mirror
Water reflects
Its surrounding

Jesus talked about
Living water

The kind
Only He can give

When we believe in Him
He invites us
To come and drink
And rivers of living water
Will flow
From within us

Then…

The world sees

Your reflection
On the water of our hearts

Your reflection
On Your living water
Flowing from within us

When we are kind to people
They see the kindness of God

When we are good to them
They see Your goodness

They see Your reflection

Like a mirror
Water reflects
Its surrounding

And rivers of living water

Reflect

You

March 11, 2022

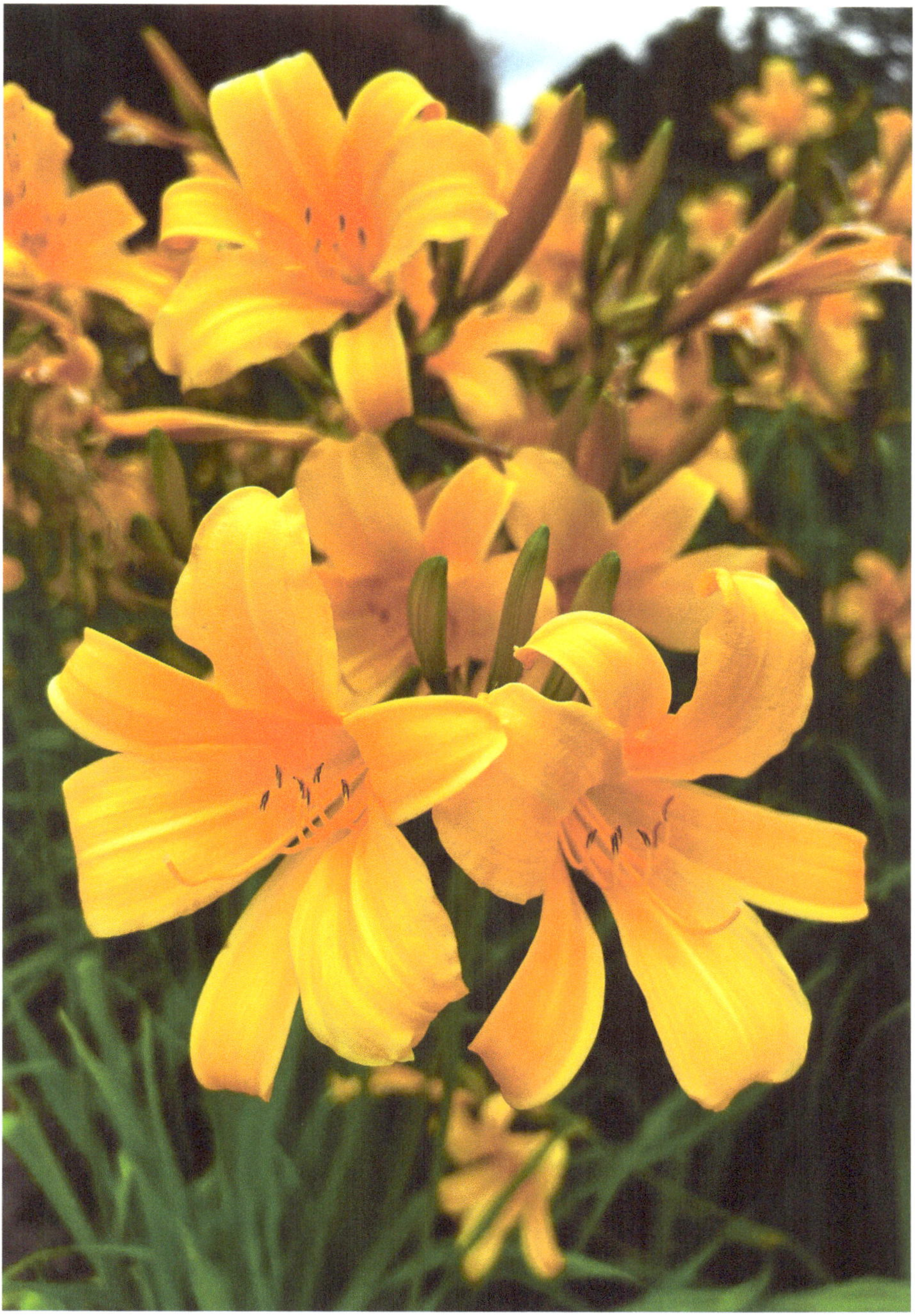

Did You choose to keep?

When I get to Heaven

When I get to see You

Your eyes
Like flames of fire...

Your face
Shining brighter than the sun...

Will I also see
The engraving?

After Your ascension...
Did You choose to keep them?

The marks of Your perfect love

When God
Gave You back
Your eternity

Did You choose to keep?
Your love for humanity
Engraved in Your skin

Jesus...

Are Your hands still pierced?

March 20, 2022

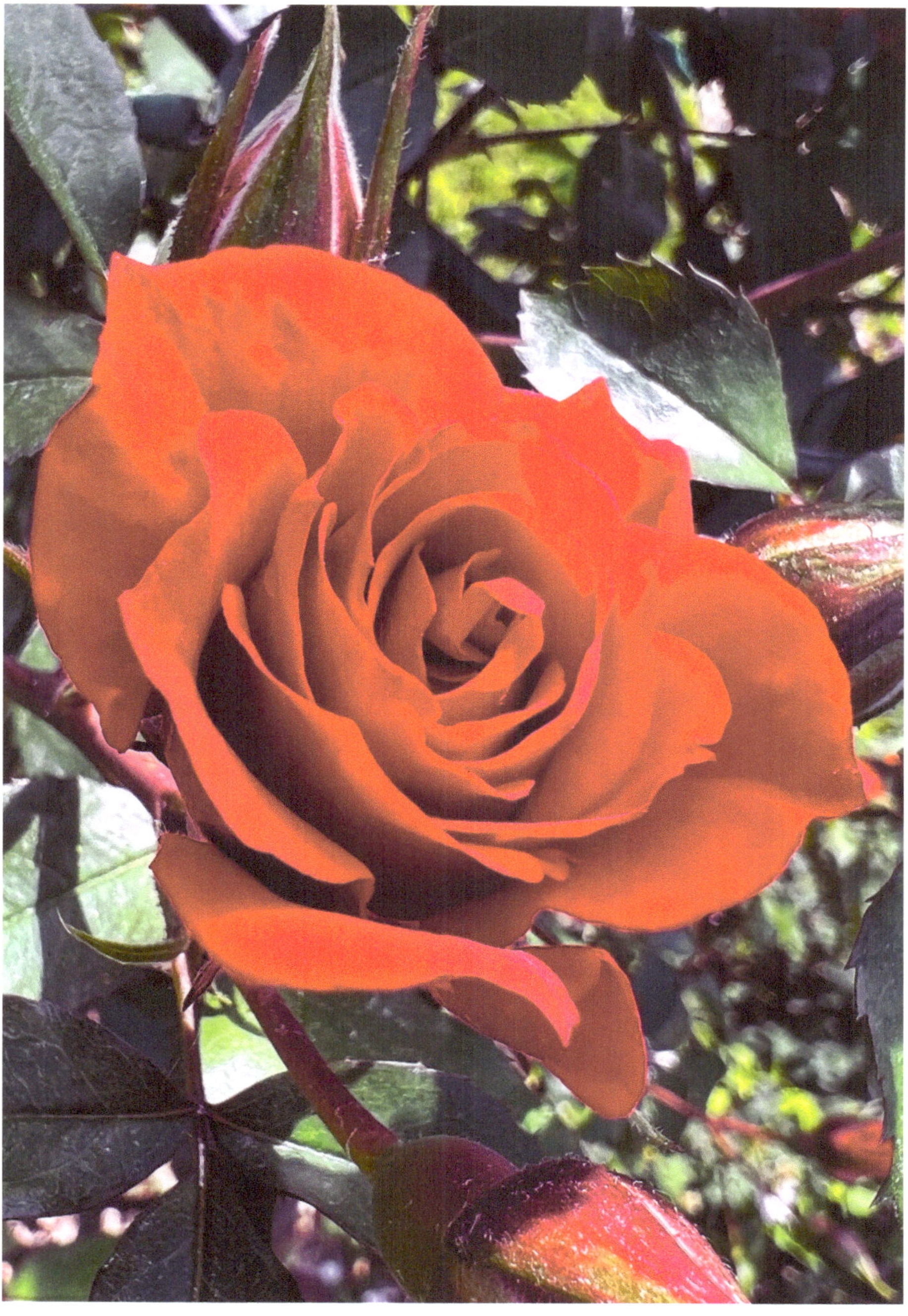

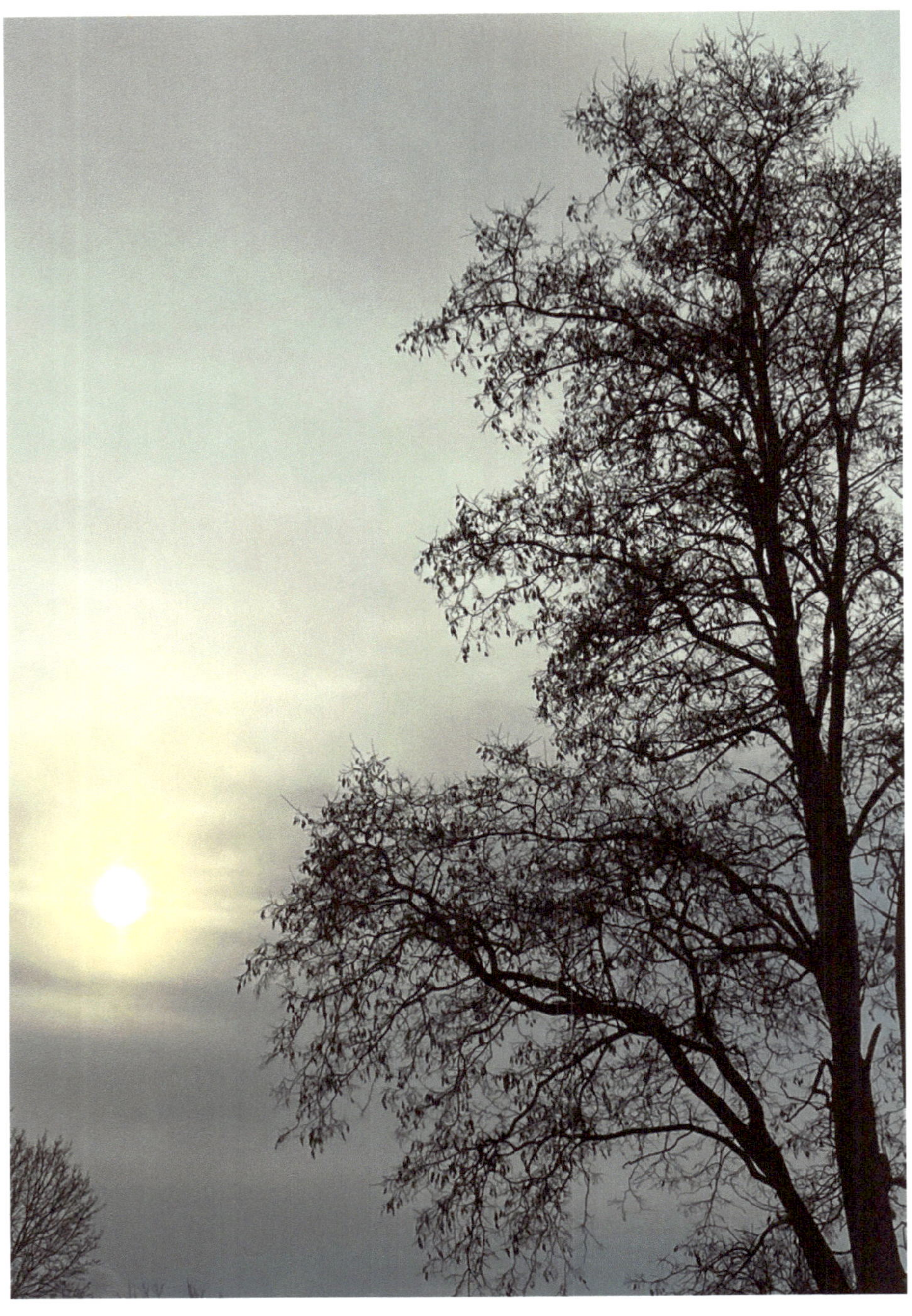

Midnight

They were upon their midnight

There was not enough time
To change the course of their lives

They were condemned...
They were dying...

Still...

They mocked
The King on the cross

Both on each side

Then...

One protested
Against the other

He knew he was guilty
He also knew
Jesus was not

With a reprimand
To silence the goat
The lost sheep
Asked Jesus to remember him when...

Not when...
But now
Today
Was the reply

They were upon their midnight
Both on each side

There was enough time
To change the end of their lives

There was enough time
To change their future

March 21, 2022

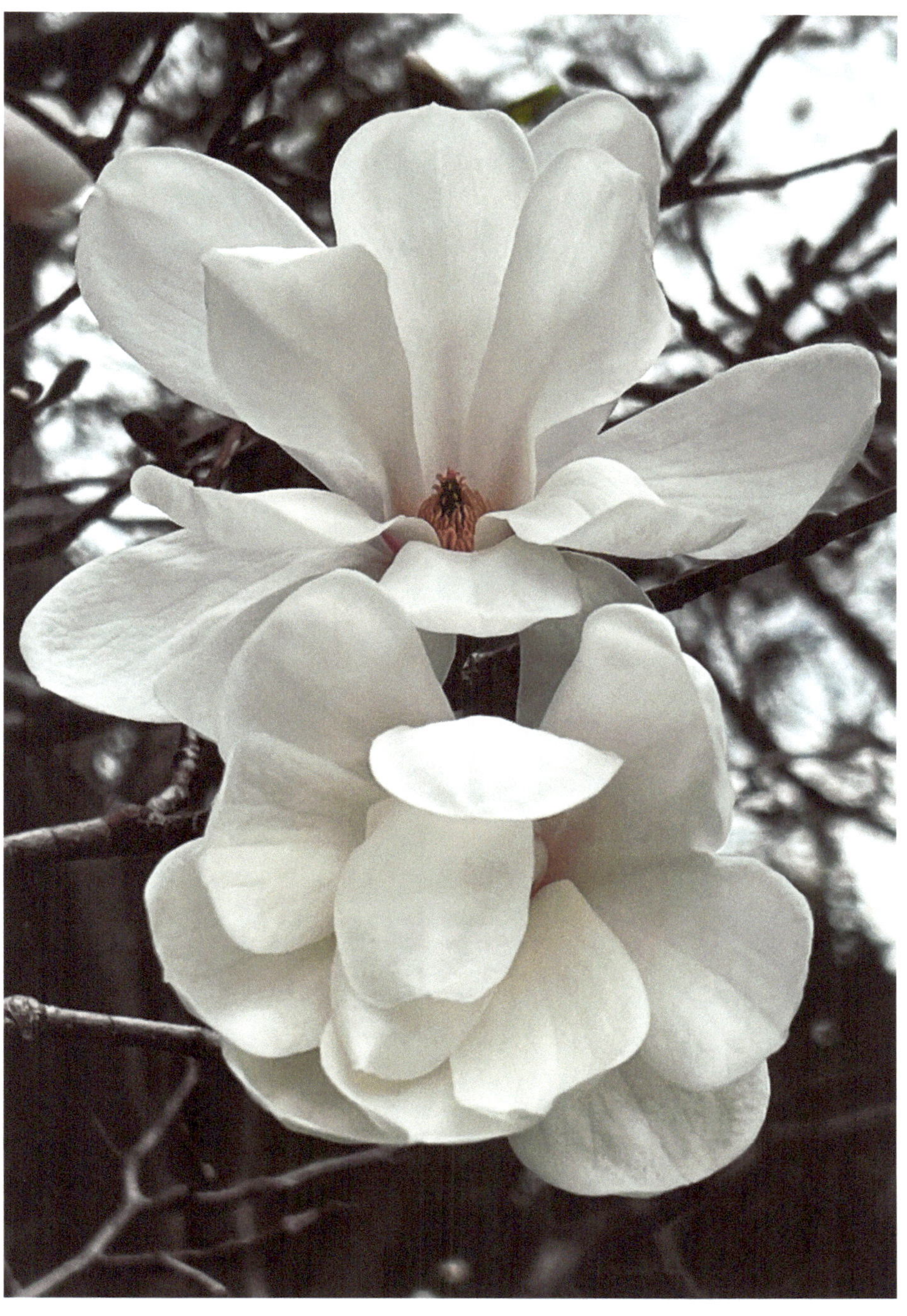

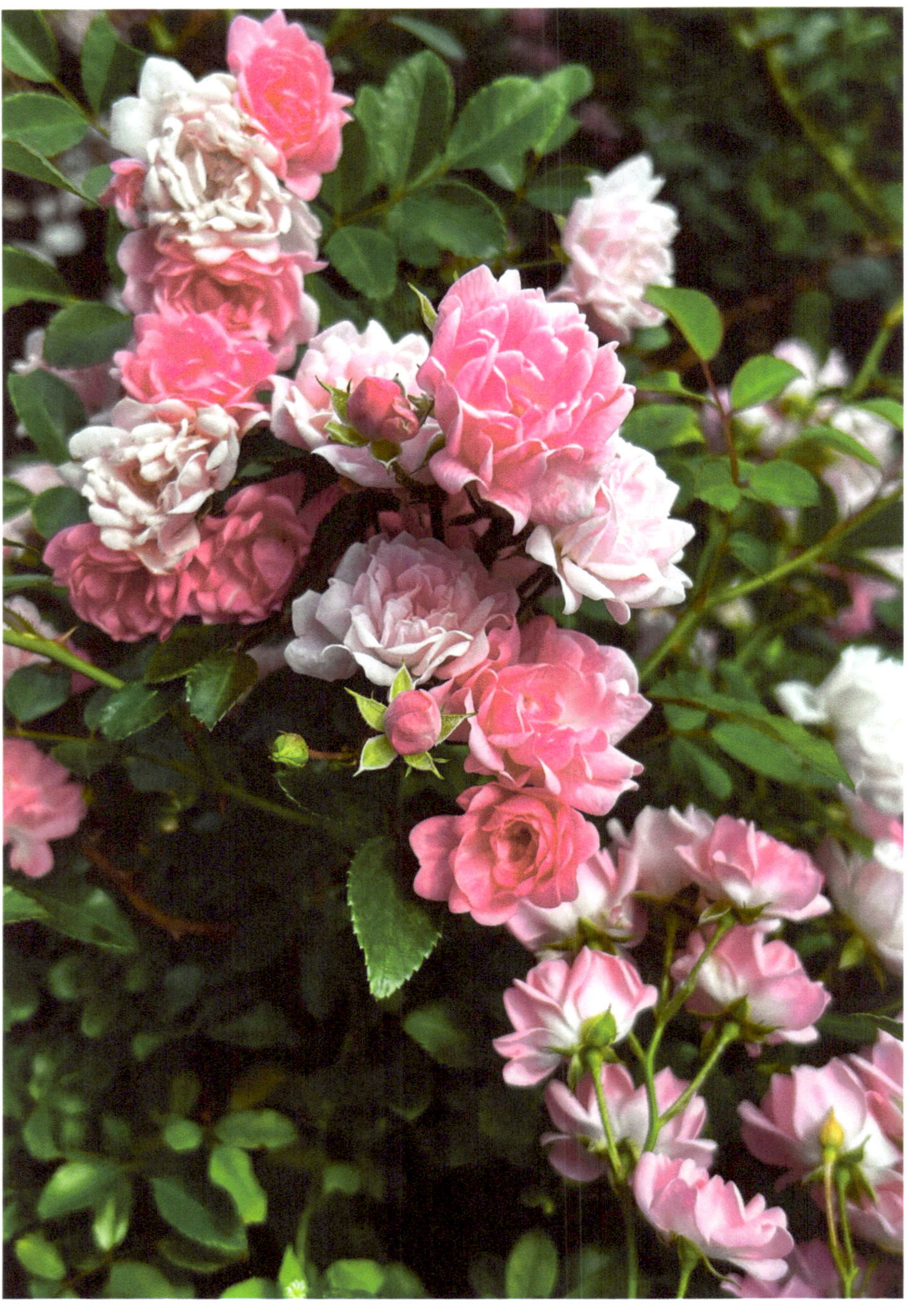

Garden

Is there a garden in your life?

A crossroads, a temptation...
A place where you must decide
To do the right thing
To trust, to forgive, to serve God...
Or go the selfish way

What do you do in your garden?

Do you ask for His guidance and His help?

Do you talk to God before you decide?

We know the outcome when we don't

Adam and Eve didn't go to God in their garden

Do you?

Jesus did

What if Eve had done the same?

What if she had brought her doubt, her dilemma
Her temptation to God?

Do you think that would have been the end of the lying, shrewd, and
deceiving serpent that day?

I do

Is there a garden in your life?

Do you go to God before you decide?

April 22, 2022

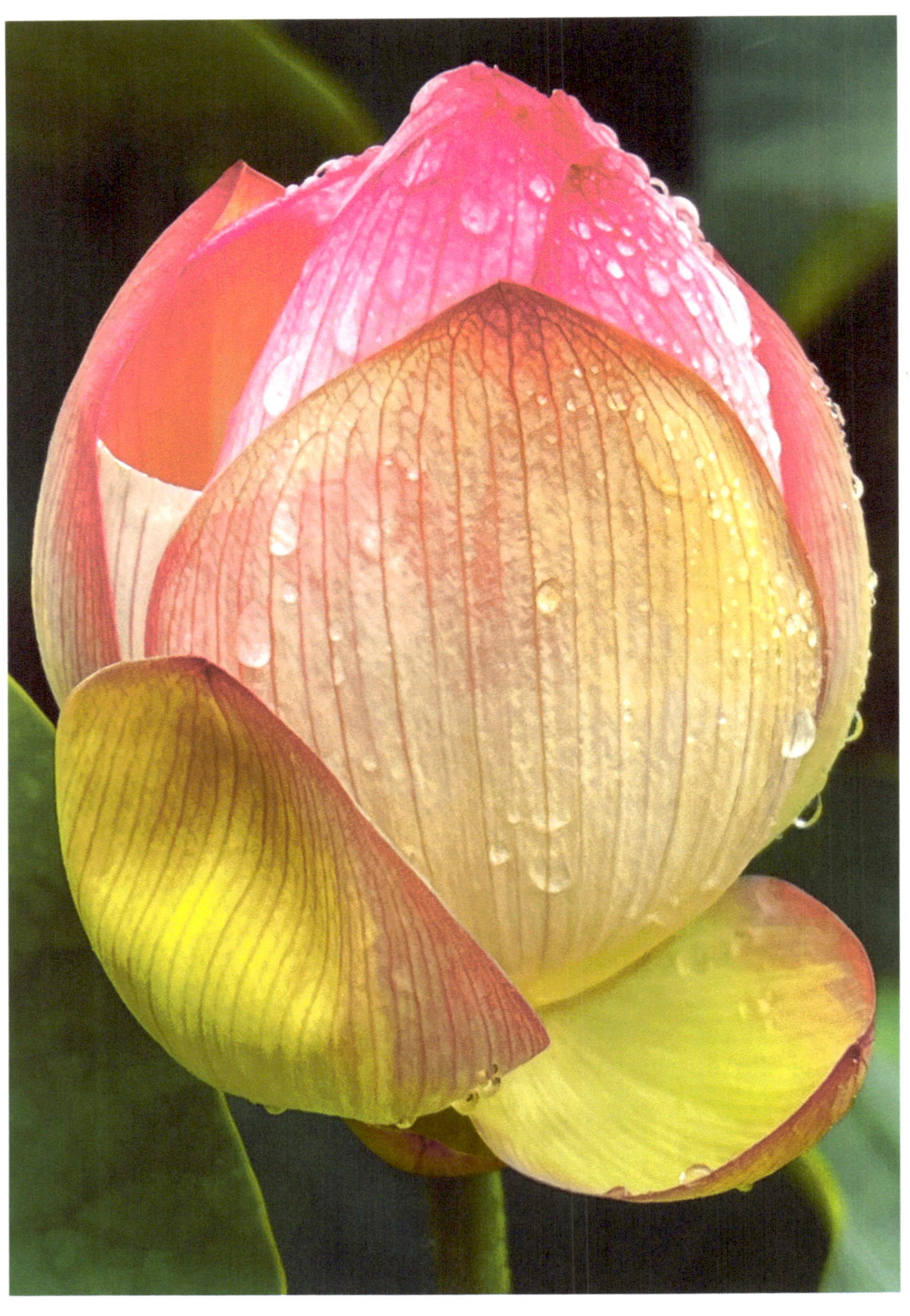

Dew

Dew
On my heart
Each morning

Infiltrating my soul
With what I need
Today

Invisible mist
Cascading from Heaven's richness
Like manna from the sky

Unimaginable goodness
Undeserved favors
Unending blessings

Perfectly crafted
From the depth of Your love

Grace

Yours

On my heart
Each morning

Infiltrating my soul
With exceedingly more
Than what I need
Today

May 26, 2022

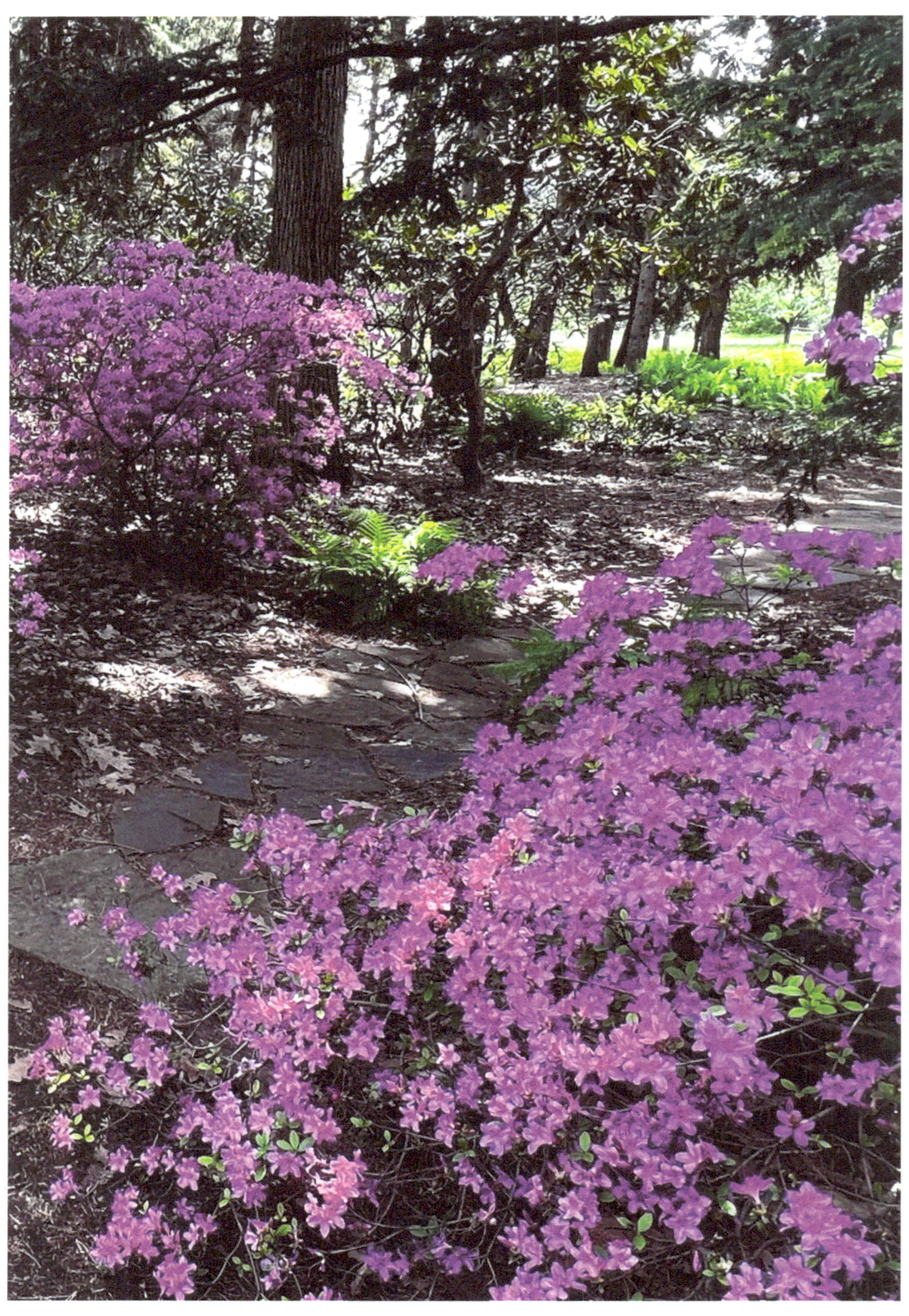

Detours

Detours
While on a road trip
Can be a pleasant surprise
Of beautiful scenery
We would have missed otherwise

But on the road of life
They are rarely welcome
And we never add them
To our agendas or lists of goals to achieve

However...I am learning to see
How important they are

Detours
Make us grow
Patience and perseverance are acquired
On a zigzagging course

We may encounter new friends
Or someone that needs our help, or the reverse
As we walk the alternate route

Perhaps they will bring forth
Hidden talents or skills
Opportunities unknown before

As I pause and look back
Important turns on my road

Detours
Are surprises
Meant to enrich our lives
Of blessings
We would have missed otherwise

June 3, 2022

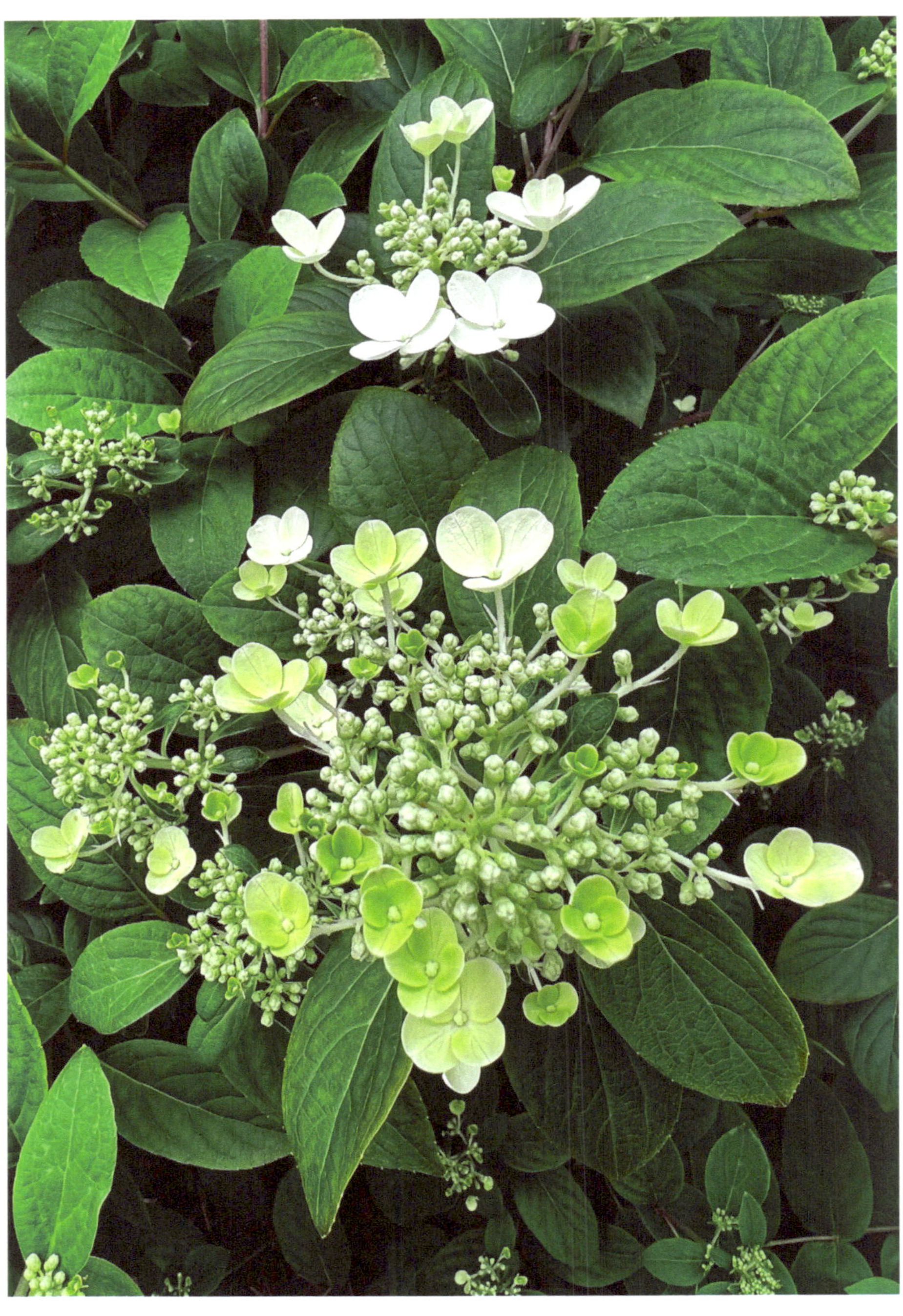

Wings

Prayers
To You

We equip them with wings
And send them on their way

Oceans and oceans of prayers
Riding the wind of our beliefs
With wings of faith
With wings of hope

Reaching Your shore
Reaching Your heart
Daily

Prayers with wings
You receive them with joy

And all will be heard

And all will be answered

With wings of Your own

Your perfect will
Your perfect love

For us

June 21, 2022

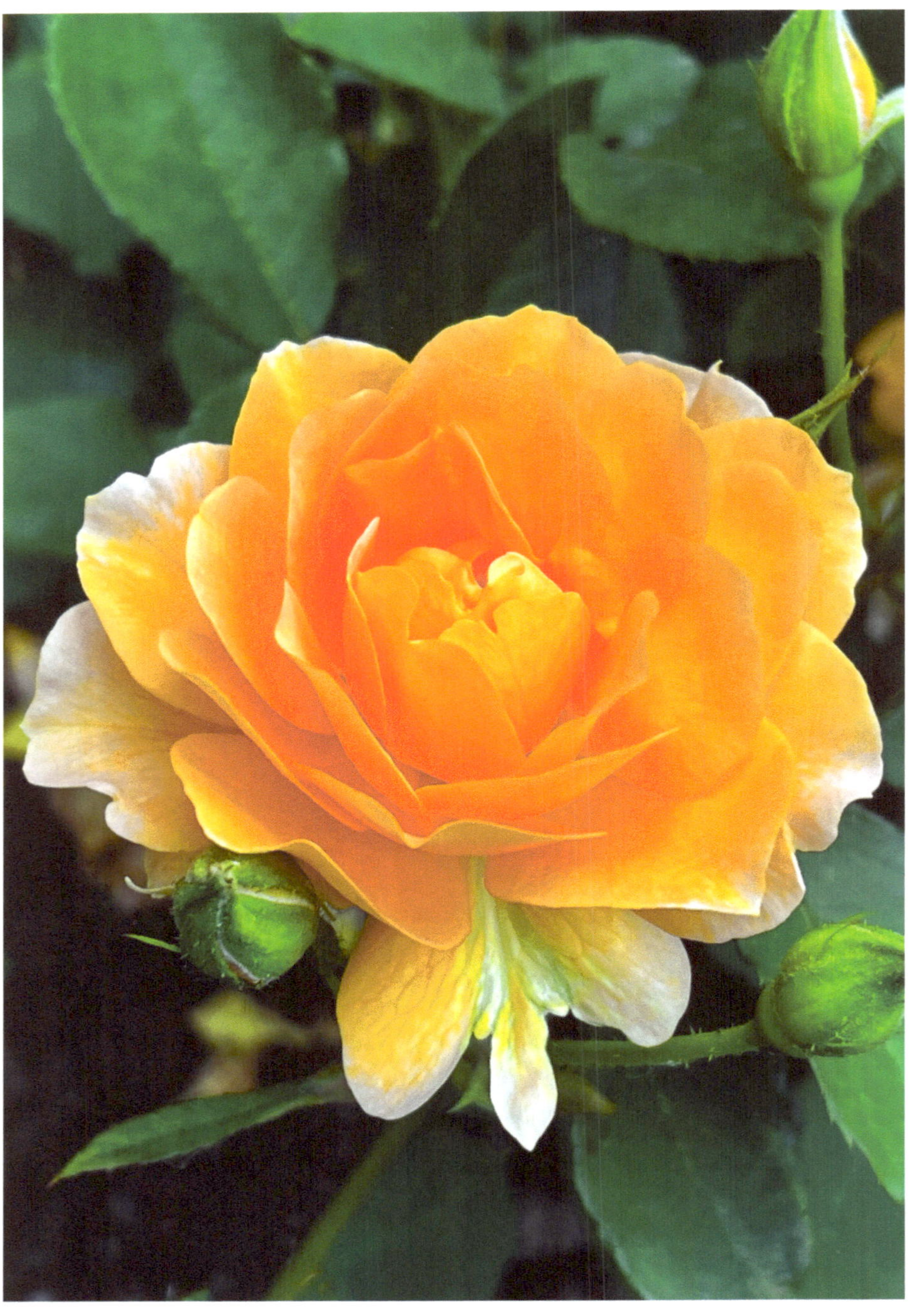

Deep within our soul

Deep within our soul
You placed a gift

Deep within the earth
You did the same

Then...
You allowed
The perfect conditions to take place

Moments of intense heat
And pressure from all sides

Moments in life
When...

The gift is tested
And purified

The carbon crystallizes

Moments in life
When...

We realize the gift is our only lifeline
We hold on to it
And refuse to let go

Moments
When...
Afterward

Deep within our soul
The gift...
Our faith in You

Has grown

And become...

Like the gift
Transformed
Within the earth

Solid
Beautiful
Unbreakable
Magnificent

A perfect stunning diamond

The strongest rock on earth

Deep within our soul

July 18, 2022

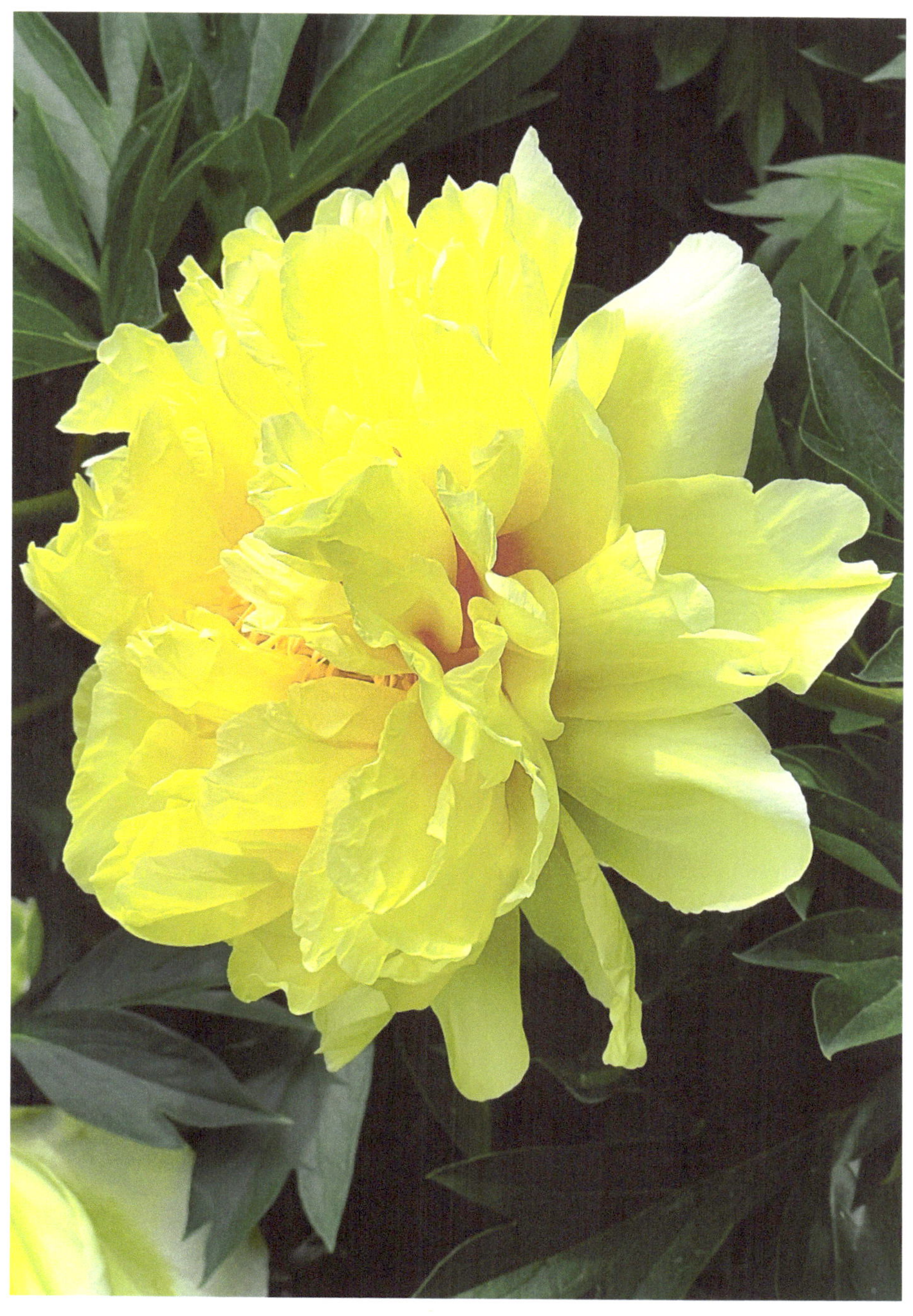

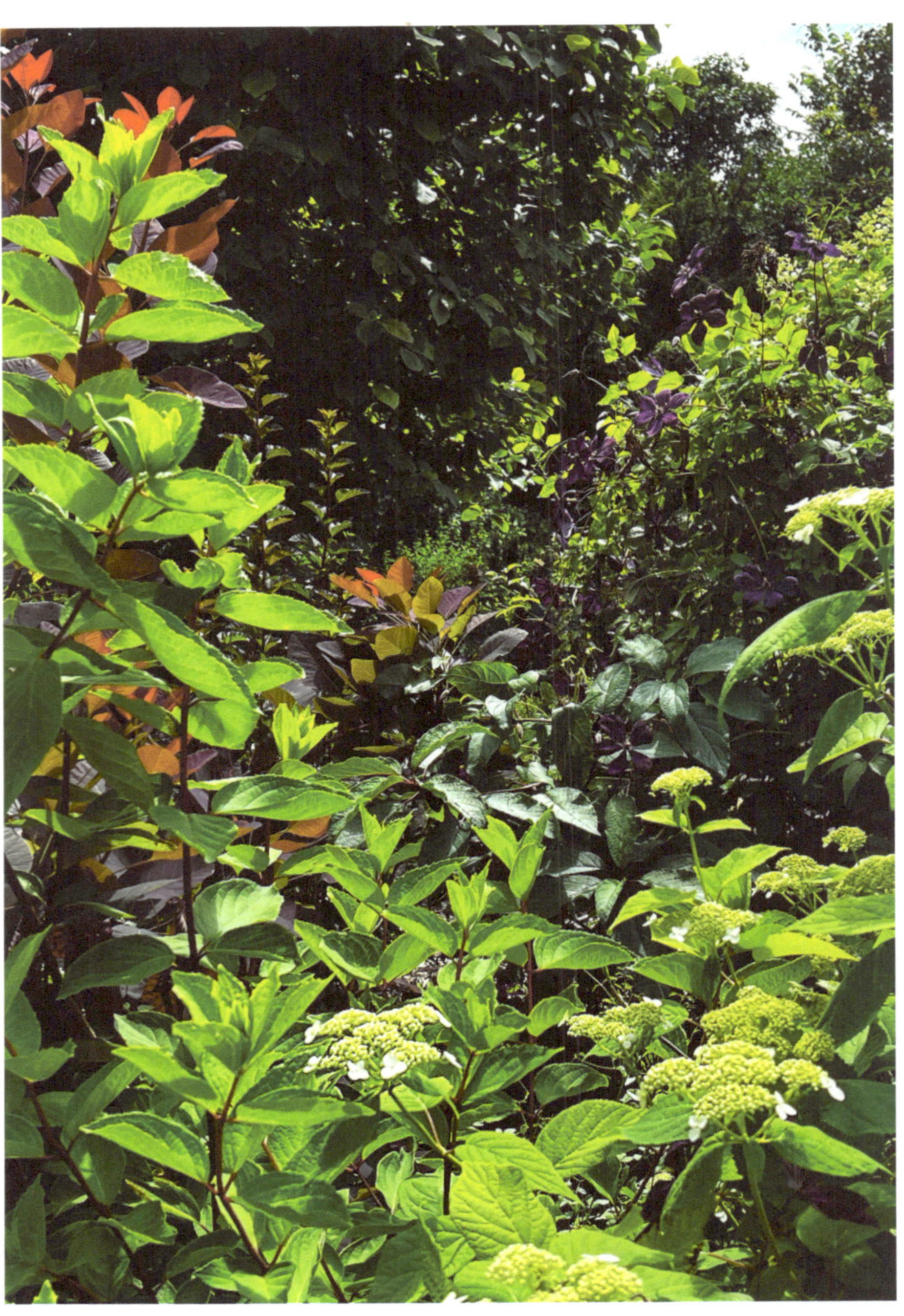

Yet You didn't

You could have...

Simply let
The green leaves
Fall to the ground

Yet You didn't

First
You draped them up
In gold, orange and red
Colourful scenery
Each year

You could have...

Created simply...

Yet You didn't

You created extravagantly
From an endless well of
Ideas and imagination

You could have...

Simply let
Humankind remain guilty
Leave us in our sinful rags
When we fell to the ground

Yet You didn't

For God so loved the world...

And You love extravagantly

First
Knowing what would happen
You made a way
For us to be draped
In a robe of righteousness

A way for us to give up our filthy rags
For clothes of salvation

You could have…

Simply let
The green leaves
Fall to the ground

Yet You didn't

And my heart
Is full of love
For You

And my heart
Overflows with gratitude
Because…

You could have…

Created simply…

Loved simply…

Yet You didn't

July 18, 2022

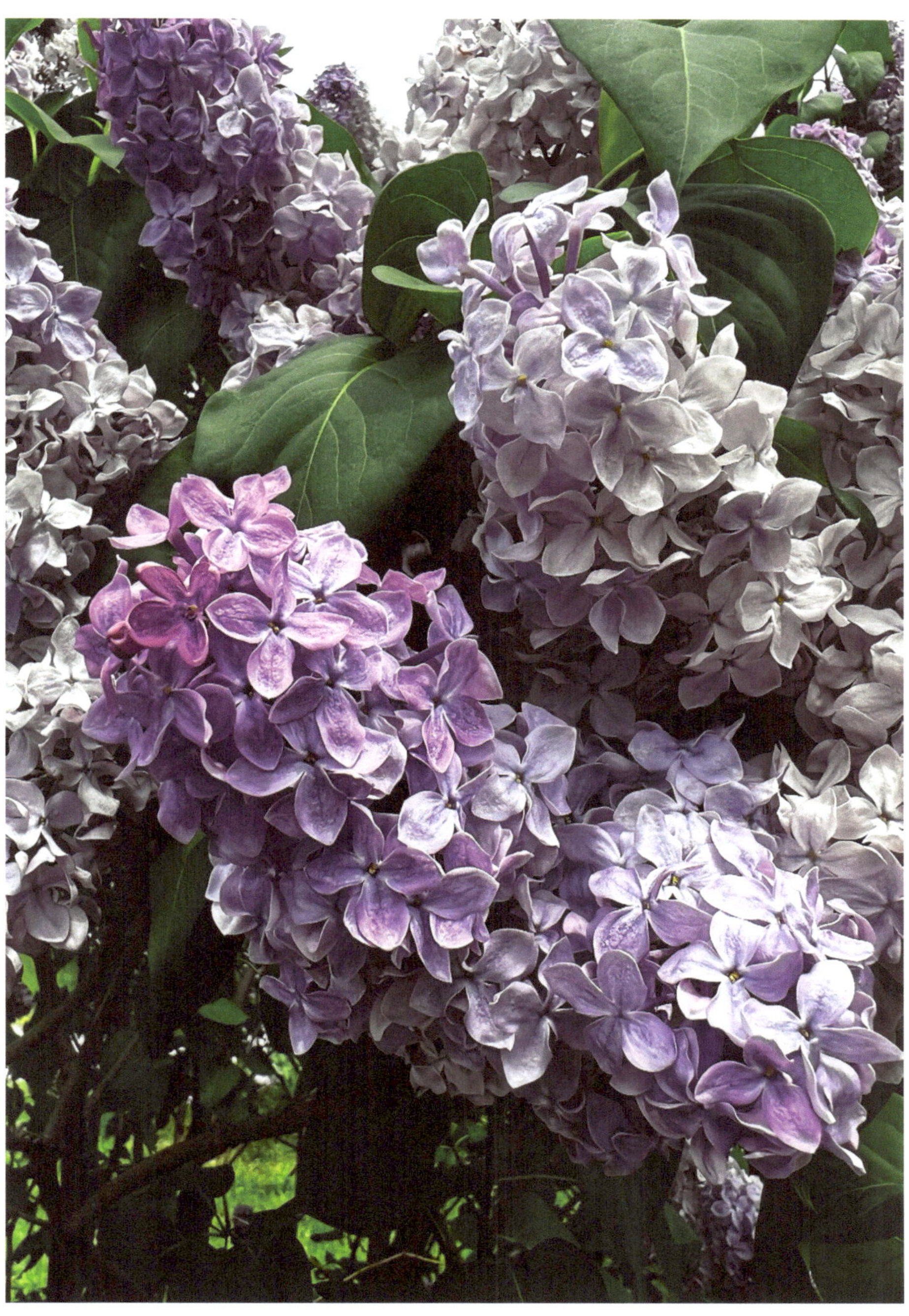

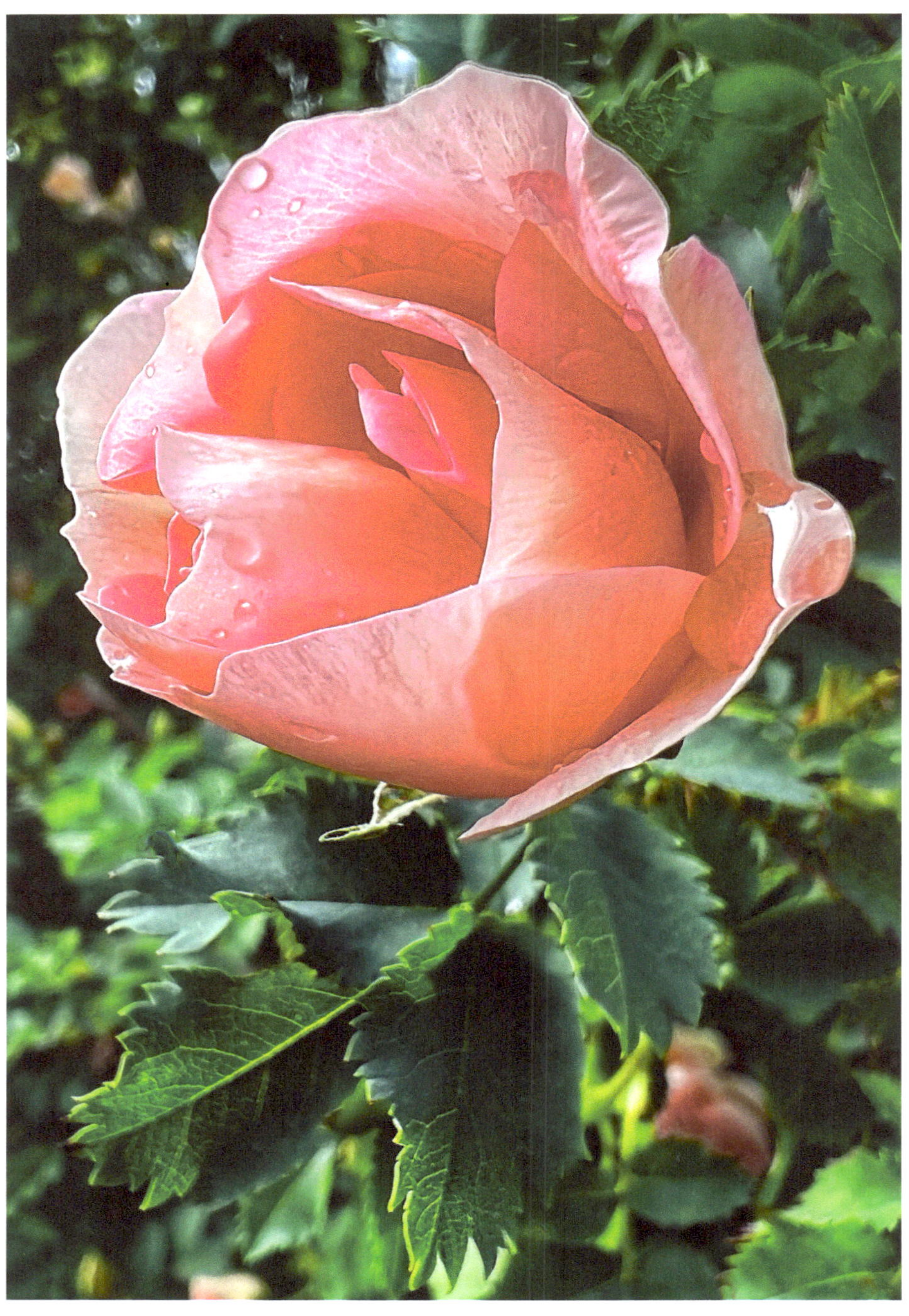

One inside the other

Visualize
Three nesting dolls

Beautifully patterned
In the same image

Skillfully designed to fit

One inside the other

Visualize
The middle one

There lies your heart

Beautifully patterned
In the same image

Skillfully designed to fit
Inside God's heart

As we abide in Him
He promised to abide in us

Entwined homes in hearts

Ours
And His

Living...

One inside the other

August 14, 2022

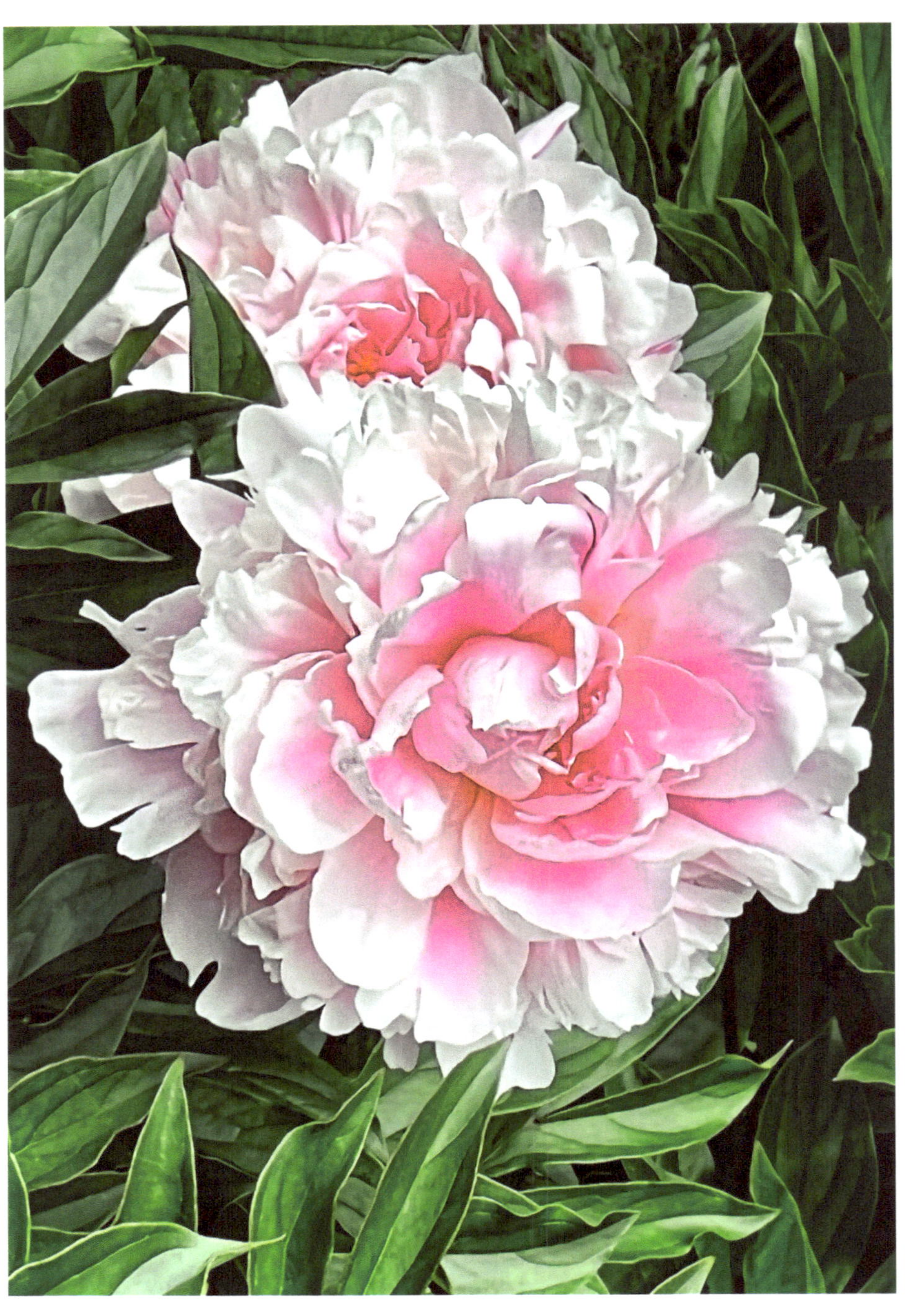

With You

In Your care
We are safe

In Your strength
We are equipped

In Your love
We are strong

In Your promise
We have eternity

And

Before we reach Heaven

You provide

Here on earth

With You

A place

Where...

Judgment remains outside
And acceptance welcomes you in

The tapestry on the wall is comfort
And serenity is all you can breathe

Your soul can rest at the end of the day...

August 17, 2022

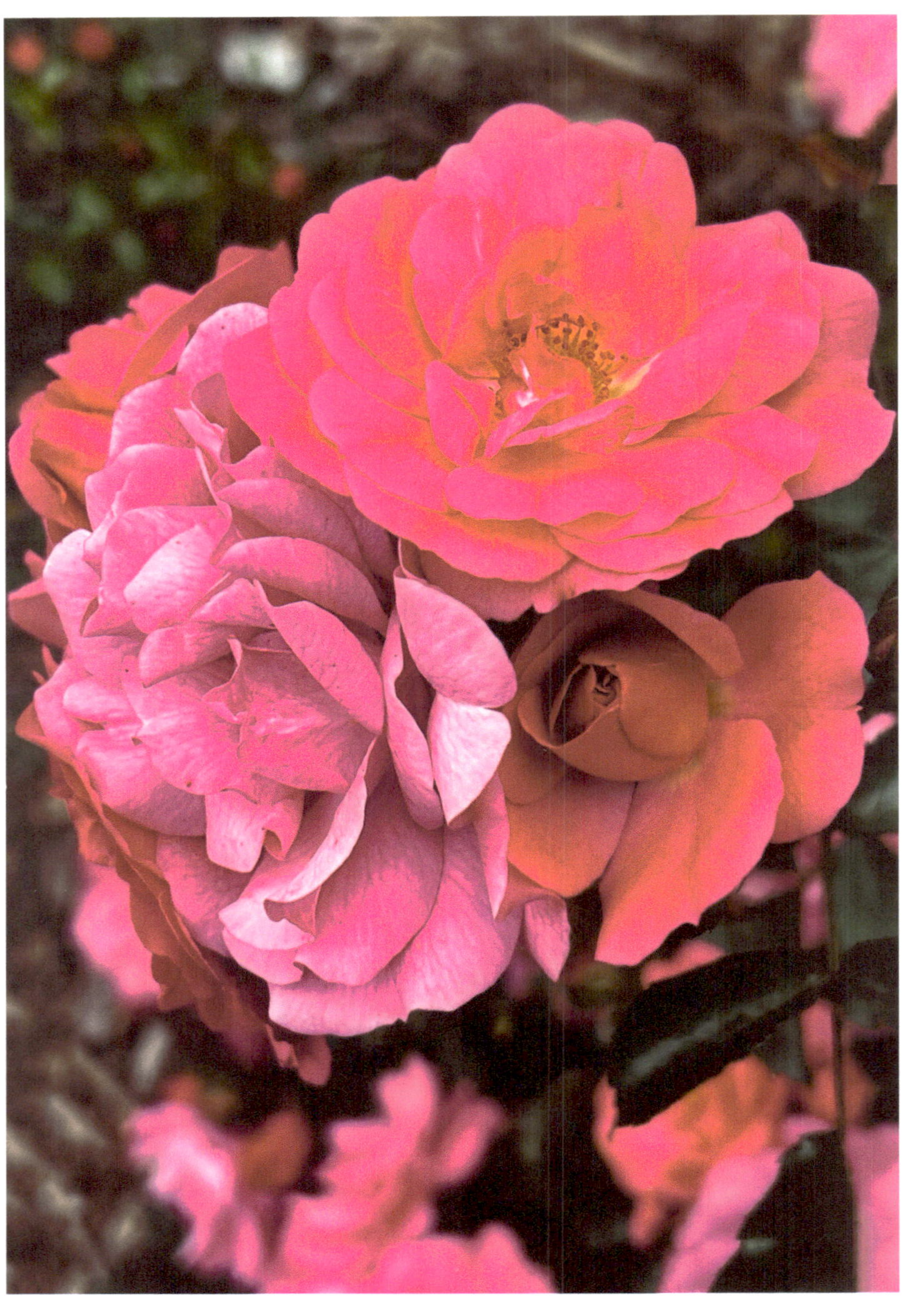